COOKING AT HOME WITH
PEDATHA

Vegetarian Recipes from a
Traditional Andhra Kitchen

Jigyasa Giri

Pratibha Jain

Transliteration scheme for pronunciation of Telugu terms:
(This is not an exhaustive Transliteration index, only a general guideline).

For the Telugu terms in this book, the vowels conform to the English phonetic sounds like *a* in *spiral*, *e* in *red*, *i* in *pin*, *o* in *polite*, *u* in *pull*.

Other pronunciation guidelines are as follows:
ā as in *father*
ē as the *a* in *lay*
ee as in *peep*
ō as in *pole*
oo as in *pool*
d as in *den*
dh as the *th* in *there*
t as in *tap*
th as the *t* in *Sita, Hindustan*

The word *Pedatha* is given the status of a proper noun in this book; to be pronounced as *Pedhathā*.

Fifth print December 2010

Cover and book design Envission Communication & Kavitha Shivan
Photographs Srivatsa Shandilya

© 2005 Jigyasa Giri & Pratibha Jain
Email write@pritya.com
Website www.pritya.com

PRITYA
70 (New), Dr. Ranga Road, Mylapore, Chennai 600004, Tamilnadu, India.

Printers Pragati Offset Pvt. Ltd., Hyderabad

ISBN-10: 81-902993-0-1
ISBN-13: 978-8190299305

"From food all creatures are produced. And all creatures that dwell on earth, by food they live and into food they finally pass. Food is the chief among beings. Verily he obtains all good who worships the Divine as food."

Taittiriya Upanishad

Pedatha, an inspiration

'Pedatha', the inspiration behind this book, is my eldest sister Subhadra Krishna Rau Parigi. Born on 2nd May, 1921 in Guntur, Andhra Pradesh, her earliest memories are of the large house in Berhampur where she grew up - especially the hustle and bustle in the kitchen. She used to love watching our mother cook with love and care to feed the large family and friends, including illustrious visitors like Gandhiji, Rajagopalachari, Gopal Reddy and others.

Our mother, Late Smt. Saraswathi Bai Giri, wife of former Indian President, Bharat Ratna Dr. V.V. Giri - was an expert cook. She was a repository of knowledge of a vast variety of Indian vegetarian cuisine. Subhadra, the eldest of a large number of eternally hungry siblings, was ideally positioned, as she modestly puts it, to imbibe the best of culinary skills from our mother.

Due to her husband late Shri Krishna Rau Parigi's official postings, Subhadra has lived in Madras, Delhi, Ceylon, Burma, and in Pondicherry (during French rule). A great host, her house was always filled with guests. While in Pondicherry and Burma as the Vice-Consul's wife, she herself used to make dishes which were thoroughly relished by locals and visiting dignitaries alike.

She currently resides in Bangalore and is the mother of four children, Saraswathi Dinesh, Rekha Ram Jayanthi, Late V.G. Parigi, and Preetham Parigi. A good conversationalist, she can fluently speak Telugu, Tamil, Kannada, Hindi and English.

Those who meet her love her, and those who eat her food admire her cooking. No wonder she has admirers all over the world.

I am flattered that Pratibha and Jigyasa have asked me, among innumerable friends and relatives, to introduce my sister.

Mrs. Sarla Surya Rao

Whose food I eat, her song I sing

The first time I heard anyone referring to my mother as 'Pedatha' was possibly in the late sixties - I must have been just over fourteen. When my cousins grew up, the word 'Pedatha' became synonymous with that aunt who was ever ready to indulge anyone who came visiting. A great believer in sharing love, she expressed her affection by cooking and serving tasty food, in traditional Andhra vegetarian style. Practically any time of the day.

We grew up in large families with several members dropping in over weekends and sometimes during weekdays. The universal belief was that you will never ever be disappointed if you get invited or invite yourself to Pedatha's home for a sumptuous meal.

It may sound strange that I grew up believing that the cooks ran the kitchen and the food arrived on the table, thanks to them. It was only later during my teens when I realized that my mother was the real chef!

I earnestly believe that every individual has a unique source of joy and energy, giving a special bounce to their life. With my mother it was, is, and will always be her penchant and passion for cooking and feeding friends and relatives.

I express my deep sense of appreciation to Jigyasa and Pratibha who in writing this book have not only put together my mother's recipes but have indeed knitted together happy memories of her life.

A.P. Parigi
Director
Bennett Coleman & Co. Ltd. (Times of India)

A tryst with tradition

A full-spirited claim by one of Subhadra Rau's nephews, "My Pedatha is the best cook in the world," became the inspiration for this book and its title. The nickname 'Pedatha' was a simpler, child's version of 'Peddha Atthayyā' which means oldest aunt (father's sister) in Telugu.

We have grown up believing that cooking is all about being quick, clever, and creative. Readymade powders, instant purees, and our freezers are now our salvation. It is remarkable; it is practical. Every generation must and does 'contemporarize'. Nevertheless, as we interacted with Pedatha, we realized that although ease has been gained in the kitchen, a certain unhurriedness as a way of life has been lost. For us, it was a peek into another time, another world, a unique kind of 'patience'.

Two years ago...

After indulging in another soul-satisfying meal at Pedatha's home in Bangalore, we re-crowned her the world's best cook. The 'Vāngi bāth' was exceptional. She smiled indulgently and simply said, "Anybody can cook that, it is so easy to make".

We didn't quite believe her until she gave us the recipe which, despite being exotic, was amazingly clear and precise. On an impulse, we switched on our laptop, and keyed in the recipe. Pedatha was amused, and happily gave us some more. Back home in Chennai, we were excited at the accuracy of her recipes every time we tried them out. After that, whenever we visited her in Bangalore, her cooking became an integral part of our conversations. And somewhere along the way what would have remained a personal collection of recipes evolved into this book.

Pedatha's culinary treasures are well-known among family and friends. This book is only the tip of the iceberg, not just of Andhra cuisine, but also of Pedatha's knowledge of it.

When it came to sharing recipes, she was always more excited about pachchadi, podi and pappu rather than idli, dosai, pesarattu or vadai. Accordingly, the contents of this book reflect her joy for sharing some of her favourite lunch and dinner-time recipes.

Of course, one thing we never questioned her about was how much time any recipe would take. We already knew her answer to that - "As long as it takes for a good dish to be ready." Though approximate timings during the various steps of the recipes have been given, preparation and cooking time have not been mentioned. "Don't look at the time, look at the pan", she once remarked.

As she spoke, we wrote, attempting to absorb her experience and her knowledge. To capture her years of wisdom in limited words of print was indeed an exciting and enriching process, albeit, no easy task. As Raimon Panikkar, the cross-cultural thinker, has aptly remarked, "Wisdom resides in the spoken rather than in the written word."

In this journey with Pedatha, our deepest gratitude and appreciation to:

Prabodh Jain for his inspiration, vision and sustained creativity throughout the project.

Kavitha Shivan, for her endless creativity with the book's design and help with the photography, Shobha Vishwanath for her 'onslaughts', Prashanthi Aysola, Prasiddha Ramarao and Sangeetha Surana, for their involvement and help at various stages.

Dr. Mohini Giri, who has always urged that Pedatha's recipes be recorded for posterity, and Mrs. Sarla Surya Rao, who with her innate warmth first initiated Jigyasa into Andhra cuisine. Preetham & Vrinda Parigi for their faith and unflinching support.

Our families, for their love and encouragement. Girish, who recognized the possibility of these recipes going beyond just a personal collection, and Mahendar for being an eager and constructive critic.

Our greatest pleasure is to present this book to Pedatha.

December 2005

Pedatha lives on...

So often the words of that old, immortal song come to mind when we revisit our journey with Pedatha – "Where do I begin to tell the story of how great a love can be, the sweet love story that is older than the sea...". She is no more in this earthly abode, but Pedatha lives on...in our kitchens and in our hearts.

How can we ever forget the day her son first launched the book in Mumbai! As the cover of the book was unveiled in the form of an 8*8 ft screen, Pedatha gazed at her face on the cover and actually put her palms together at the sheer magnificence of it. To see her joyfully sign book after book with untiring excitement till her last breath, to hear her say that this book had made her a model without walking the ramp, to hear from her son that it gave her a burst of energy in the sunset of her life makes it worth every effort, every risk that we took.

Our heartfelt thanks for the love and appreciation we have received from readers world over, to all those who say that with this book, they have rediscovered their grandmothers in their kitchens. For us, it simply reiterates our faith in working from the heart and in our belief that if you don't take the shortcut, you will go a long way.

December 2009
Jigyasa & Pratibha

>> *All recipes in this book serve approximately six adults, except chutneys, powders and crispies which are usually preserved for longer periods.*

>> *General measures used in this book: teaspoon (5 ml), tablespoon (15 ml) and cup (200 ml) approximately.*

CHUTNEYS *Pachchadi*

POWDERS *Podi*

RICE *Annam*

VEGETABLES *Koora*

DALS *Pappu, Chāru*

YOGURT *Perugu*

SWEETS *Theepi*

CRISPIES *Vadiyālu*

Andhra pachchadis are spicy chutneys to be mixed into rice with a dollop of ghee. However, you may also enjoy them as a spread on toast, or as an accompaniment with idlis, dosais and chapatis. They are mostly ground into a paste, but in some like Theeya dhōsakāya pulusu pachchadi and Carrot pachchadi, the vegetables are chopped, but not ground. Eaten either cold or at room temperature, most of these chutneys can be preserved for a week or more in the refrigerator.

The best way to mix a pachchadi into rice as done in South India is with your palm and fingers working in precise unison. For those of you not accustomed to such a practice, it might seem rather strange. But do give it a try. Who knows! You might just discover the absolutely delightful manner of feeding your loved ones with this hand-made ball of rice and pachchadi - famously known as 'muddha', just as Pedatha does so warmly. And don't forget that dollop of ghee!

SPINACH CHUTNEY *Pālakoora Pachchadi* *pic. p. 18*

blended with spices, spinach takes on an interesting twist

Spinach (or Amaranth leaves) *2 bunches*
Thick tamarind pulp *2 tbsps*
Sesame seeds *2 tsps*
Oil *4 tsps*
Salt *to taste*

The 1st tempering
Split black gram (husked) *1 tbsp*
Mustard seeds *2 tsps*
Fenugreek seeds *¼ tsp*
Red chillies *6-8, nicked at tail with stalks retained*
Green chillies *4-5, whole with stalks removed*
Curry leaves *10-12, with stem*
Asafoetida powder or paste *1 tsp*

The 2nd tempering
Split black gram (husked) *1 tsp*
Mustard seeds *1 tsp*

1   Chop spinach roughly along with the tender stems. This should amount to about 6 cups after chopping.

2   Dry roast the sesame seeds on a low flame until golden brown and grind to a coarse powder. Refer to Pedatha's tip (p. 82) for the correct method of powdering sesame.

3   Heat 1 tsp oil in a wok, add the spinach, cover and simmer for at least 10 minutes. When the spinach is well cooked and the water has evaporated completely, switch off the flame and set aside.

4   In another wok, heat 2 tsps oil for the 1st tempering. Add the gram; as it turns golden, add the mustard and then the fenugreek. Switch off the flame and with the browning of the fenugreek, add the red chillies. As they turn bright red, stir in the green chillies, curry leaves and asafoetida powder.

5   Grind this tempering along with the tamarind pulp, powdered sesame and salt into a fine paste. Do not add water while grinding. Now add the cooked spinach and grind coarsely.

6   Heat the remaining oil for the 2nd tempering. Add the gram; as it turns golden, pop the mustard and switch off the flame. Garnish the pachchadi with this crunchy tempering.

Serve with steamed rice and a dollop of ghee.

VARIATION
RIDGE GOURD CHUTNEY
Beerakāya Pachchadi
Substitute spinach with 4-5 ridge gourds. Peel gourds if skins are not tender.

BRINJAL CHUTNEY *Vankāya Pachchadi*

a lip-smacking experience

Brinjal (bharta variety) *1 large*
Tamarind pulp *2 tbsps*
Oil *2½ tsps*
Salt *to taste*

The tempering
Split black gram (husked) *1 tbsp*
Mustard seeds *2 tsps*
Fenugreek seeds *¼ tsp*
Red chillies *6-8, nicked at tail with stalks retained*
Green chillies *3-4, whole with stalks removed*
Curry leaves *10-12, with stem*
Coriander leaves *½ cup, chopped roughly*
Asafoetida powder or paste *1 tsp*

Serve with steamed rice and a dollop of ghee.

Pedatha says...

Enhance the flavour of this dish with cucumber. Take ½ cup of finely chopped cucumber, squeeze out the water and mix into the pachchadi.

1   Coat the brinjal lightly with oil and roast directly on a low flame till the skin turns black an starts cracking. Pierce with a fork to make sure the brinjal is well cooked. Scrape off the skin, mash well with a fork and set aside.

2   In a wok, heat the remaining oil for tempering. Add the gram; as it turns golden, add the mustard and then the fenugreek. Switch off the flame and with the browning of the fenugreek, add the red chillies. As they turn bright red, stir in the remaining ingredients for tempering.

3   Grind this tempering along with the tamarind pulp and salt into a coarse paste. Do not add water while grinding.

4   Add this paste to the brinjal pulp and mix well.

MILKY BRINJAL CHUTNEY *Iguru Pachchadi*

a cool change from the other pachchadis

Brinjal (bharta variety) *1 large*
Milk *½ cup, boiled and cooled*
Oil *1 tbsp*
Salt *to taste*

The tempering
Split black gram (husked) *¾ tsp*
Mustard seeds *½ tsp*
Green chillies *2-3, slit*
Ginger *½ tsp, grated*
Coriander leaves *1 tbsp, chopped fine*
Curry leaves *6-7, with stem*

Pedatha says...

1. Take care to use only tender brinjal as it does not have too many seeds and is easy to mash.

2. You can also make this dish using small brinjals. Instead of roasting them over a flame, chop them, cover and cook in a little oil until well done. Mash and proceed from step 2.

1   Coat the brinjal with a little oil and roast directly on low flame till the skin turns black and starts cracking. Pierce with a fork to make sure the brinjal is well cooked. Scrape off the skin and mash the pulp well with a fork.

2   When the pulp has cooled, add the milk and mix well. Set aside.

3   In a wok, heat the oil for tempering. Add the gram; as it turns golden, pop the mustard. Switch off the flame and add the remaining ingredients for tempering.

4   Mix this tempering into the pulp. Add salt just before serving so that the milk does not curdle.

Serve as a side dish in a meal.

MELON CUCUMBER CHUTNEY *Nakka Dhōsakāya Pachchadi*

the crunch of cucumber makes all the difference

Melon cucumber (Indian variety) *1 large*
Thick tamarind pulp *2 tbsps*
Oil *1 tbsp*
Salt *to taste*

The 1st tempering
Split black gram (husked) *1 tbsp*
Mustard seeds *2 tsps*
Red chillies *5-6, nicked at tail with stalks retained*
Green chillies *3-4, whole with stalks removed*
Curry leaves *10-12, with stem*
Coriander leaves *¼ cup, chopped roughly*
Asafoetida powder or paste *1 tsp*

The 2nd tempering
Mustard seeds *¼ tsp*
Asafoetida powder or paste *¼ tsp*

1   Peel the vegetable, seed and dice into ¼ inch cubes. This should amount to about 2 cups.

2   In a wok, heat 2 tsps oil for the 1st tempering. Add the gram; as it turns golden, pop the mustard. Switch off the flame and add the red chillies. As they turn bright red, stir in the remaining ingredients for tempering.

3   Grind this tempering along with the tamarind pulp, salt and a spoonful of the chopped vegetable into a coarse paste. Do not add water while grinding.

4   Transfer to a bowl and add the rest of the chopped vegetable.

5   Heat the remaining oil for the 2nd tempering. Pop the mustard; switch off the flame and add the asafoetida. Garnish the pachchadi with this tempering.

Serve with steamed rice and a dollop of ghee.

> ### Pedatha says...
> *Squeeze out water from the vegetable after chopping; this will help preserve the chutney for a few days.*

CUCUMBER SWEET AND SOUR CHUTNEY *Theeya Dhōsakāya Pulusu Pachchadi*

an easy to make dish that leaves you licking your fingers

Cucumber *2 medium*
Thick tamarind pulp *3 tbsps*
Turmeric powder *½ tsp*
Sāmbār podi (p. 28) *2 tsps*
Sesame seeds *1½ tsps*
Jaggery *1 heaped tbsp*
Coriander leaves *2 tbsps, chopped fine*
Oil *1 tbsp*
Salt *to taste*

The tempering

Split black gram (husked) *1 heaped tsp*
Mustard seeds *1 heaped tsp*
Red chillies *2-3, nicked at tail with stalks retained*
Green chillies *2, slit with stalks removed*
Curry leaves *5-7, with stem*
Asafoetida powder or paste *¼ tsp*

1 Peel the cucumber and chop into thin, 1 inch long pieces or ½ inch cubes.

2 Dry roast the sesame seeds on a low flame until golden and grind to a coarse powder. Refer to Pedatha's tip (p. 82) for the correct method of powdering sesame.

3 Heat the oil in a wok for tempering. Add the gram; as it turns golden, pop the mustard. Lower the flame and add the chillies, curry leaves and asafoetida.

4 Add the chopped cucumber and stir for a minute. Now add the tamarind pulp, turmeric powder, sāmbār podi, powdered sesame seeds and jaggery. Cover and cook for just a few minutes.

5 Add salt just before switching off the flame. Garnish with coriander leaves.

Serve as a side dish in a meal.

VARIATIONS

Gummadikāya Pulusu Pachchadi
Follow the above recipe using sweet pumpkin instead of cucumber.

Vankāya Pulusu Pachchadi
Take a large brinjal, coat with a little oil and roast directly on low flame till the skin turns black and starts cracking. Pierce with a fork to make sure the brinjal is well cooked. Scrape off the skin and mash the pulp well with a fork. Follow the above recipe adding the cooked brinjal in the end.

WITH SMALL BRINJALS
Quarter the brinjals. Cook in a little oil until soft. Sprinkle water while cooking if required. Follow the above recipe adding the cooked brinjals in the end.

CURRY LEAF CHUTNEY *Karivēpāku Pachchadi*

choose fresh tender leaves for this blend of nutrition and flavour

Curry leaves *2 cups*
Thick tamarind pulp *3 tbsps*
Jaggery (optional) *1 tbsp*
Oil *4 tbsps*
Salt *to taste*

The 1st tempering
Split black gram (husked) *1½ tbsps*
Mustard seeds *1 tbsp*
Cumin seeds *1 tsp*
Red chillies *8-10, nicked at tail with stalks retained*
Asafoetida powder or paste *1 tsp*
Turmeric powder *½ tsp*
Coriander leaves *1 cup, chopped roughly*

The 2nd tempering
Split black gram (husked) *½ tsp*
Mustard seeds *½ tsp*

1   Wash the curry leaves and pat dry. Heat 2 tbsps oil in a wok and on a low flame, roast the curry leaves until crisp. Take care to see that they remain green. Set aside.

2   In another wok, heat 1½ tbsps oil for the 1st tempering. Add the gram; as it turns golden, add the mustard and then the cumin. Switch off the flame and add the red chillies. As they turn bright red, stir in the remaining ingredients of the 1st tempering.

3   Grind this tempering along with the curry leaves, tamarind pulp, jaggery and salt into a coarse paste. Do not add water while grinding.

4   Heat the remaining oil for the 2nd tempering. Add the gram; as it turns golden, pop the mustard. Garnish the pachchadi with this crunchy tempering.

Serve with idlis, dosas or mix into steamed rice.

Pedatha says...
If you wish to preserve this pachchadi for a longer period, avoid the coriander leaves.

GINGER CHUTNEY *Allam Pachchadi*

for those who love ginger

Ginger *1 cup, grated*
Tamarind pulp *3 tbsps*
Jaggery *1 tbsp*
Ghee *2 tbsps*
Oil *2 tbsps*
Salt *to taste*

The 1st tempering
Split black gram (husked) *1½ tbsps*
Mustard seeds *1 tbsp*
Red chillies *3-4, nicked at tail with stalks retained*
Curry leaves *½ cup*
Coriander leaves (optional) *1 cup, torn roughly*
Asafoetida powder or paste *1 tsp*
Turmeric powder *½ tsp*

The 2nd tempering
Split black gram (husked) *½ tsp*
Mustard seeds *½ tsp*

1   In a wok, heat the ghee and fry the grated ginger well for 4-5 minutes. Take care to see that the ginger turns light red in colour. Do not over-cook as the ginger must retain some of its juice. Set aside.

2   In another wok, heat 1½ tbsps oil for the 1st tempering. Add the gram; as it turns golden, pop the mustard. Switch off the flame and add the red chillies. As they turn bright red, stir in the remaining ingredients of the 1st tempering.

3   Grind this tempering along with tamarind pulp, jaggery and salt into a coarse paste. Do not add water while grinding. Now add the cooked ginger and grind coarsely.

4   Heat the remaining oil for the 2nd tempering. Add the gram; as it turns golden, pop the mustard and switch off the flame. Garnish the pachchadi with this crunchy tempering.

Serve with idlis, dosas or mix into steamed rice.

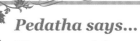

Pedatha says...
If you wish to preserve this pachchadi for a longer period, avoid the coriander leaves.

COCONUT CHUTNEY *Kobbarikāya Pachchadi*

a fiery experience - the famous brown chutney

Coconut *1 cup, grated fine*
Thick tamarind pulp *1½ tbsps*
Jaggery or sugar (optional) *1 tsp*
Oil *1 tbsp*
Salt *to taste*

The 1st tempering
Split black gram (husked) *1 heaped tsp*
Mustard seeds *1 tsp*
Fenugreek seeds *¼ tsp*
Red chillies *8-10, nicked at tail with stalks retained*
Green chillies *3-4, whole with stalks removed*
Curry leaves *6-8, with stem*
Coriander leaves *1 tbsp, chopped*
Asafoetida powder or paste *1 tsp*

The 2nd tempering
Split black gram (husked) *¼ tsp*
Mustard seeds *¼ tsp*
Asafoetida powder or paste *¼ tsp*

Serve with idlis, dosas or mix into steamed rice with a dollop of ghee.

1   In a wok, heat 2 tsps oil for the 1st tempering. Add the gram; as it turns golden, add the mustard and then the fenugreek. Switch off the flame and with the browning of the fenugreek, add the red chillies. As they turn bright red, stir in the remaining ingredients of the 1st tempering.

2   Grind this tempering along with the coconut, tamarind pulp, jaggery and salt into a coarse paste. Do not add water while grinding.

3   Heat the remaining oil for the 2nd tempering. Add the gram; as it turns golden, pop the mustard. Switch off the flame and add the asafoetida. Garnish the pachchadi with this crunchy tempering.

ONION CHUTNEY *Ullipāya Pachchadi*

a 'must try' recipe

Onions *3 large, chopped roughly*
Ginger (optional) *2 inch piece, grated*
Thick tamarind pulp *2 tbsps*
Oil *1 tbsp*
Salt *to taste*

The tempering

Split black gram (husked) *1 tbsp*
Mustard seeds *2 tsps*
Fenugreek seeds *¼ tsp*
Red chillies *8-10, nicked at tail with stalks retained*
Green chillies *3-4, whole with stalks removed*
Coriander leaves *½ cup, torn roughly*
Curry leaves *6-8, with stem*
Asafoetida powder or paste *1 tsp*

Pedatha says...

Add a medium-sized tomato, chopped and roasted in oil along with the onions for a tasty variation.

1   In a wok, heat the oil for tempering. Add the gram; as it turns golden, add the mustard and then the fenugreek. Lower the flame and with the browning of the fenugreek, add the red chillies. As they turn bright red, stir in the remaining ingredients for tempering.

2   Add the onions and ginger. Roast for 4-5 minutes until the raw smell of onion disappears.

3   Grind along with the tamarind pulp and salt into a coarse paste. Do not add water while grinding.

Serve with idlis, dosas or mix into steamed rice with a dollop of ghee.

SPICY CARROT CHUTNEY *Carrot Pachchadi*

an unusual way of enjoying carrots, as the mustard stuns your senses

Carrots *3, large*
Lemon juice *squeezed from 2 large lemons*
Oil *2 tsps*
Salt *to taste*

The tempering
Mustard seeds *¾ tsp*
Fenugreek seeds *½ tsp*
Asafoetida powder or paste *¾ tsp*

The paste
Red chillies *20-25 (or less, depending on how adventurous you dare to be!)*
Mustard seeds *½ cup*

Serve with curd rice or as an accompaniment to a meal.

Pedatha says...

Add finely chopped mango-ginger (zeodary) or raw mango to the carrot pachchadi for a tasty variation. Reduce the quantity of carrots accordingly. Add more lemon juice if you like it tangier.

1   Dice the carrots into ¼ cm bits. This should amount to about 2½ cups.

2   For the paste, soak the chillies and mustard in 1 cup water for 3-4 hours. Alternately, soak for 1 hour in hot water. Strain and grind into a fine paste, using as little of the strained water as necessary.

3   In a wok, heat the oil for tempering. Pop the mustard and then add the fenugreek. Switch off the flame and with the browning of the fenugreek, add the asafoetida.

4   Add the carrots, lemon juice, the paste and salt.

5   Store in an airtight container. This pachchadi tastes best after a day or two when the mustard flavour has soaked in well. Stays fresh for weeks in the refrigerator.

GREEN GRAM CHUTNEY *Pesarapappu Pachchadi*

a wholesome way to relish green gram without cooking it

Green gram (husked) *1 cup*
Cucumber *1 small*
Coconut *½ cup, grated*
Coriander leaves *½ cup, chopped roughly*
Garlic (optional) *5-6 flakes*
Lemon juice *2-3 tsps*
Oil *1 tbsp*
Salt *to taste*

The 1st tempering
Mustard seeds *½ tbsp*
Cumin seeds *¼ tsp*
Red chillies *8-10, nicked at tail with stalks retained*
Green chillies *5-6, whole with stalks removed*
Curry leaves *8-10, with stem*
Asafoetida powder or paste *1 heaped tsp*

The 2nd tempering
Mustard seeds *1 tsp*
Cumin seeds *1 tsp*
Curry leaves *4-5, with stem*

1   Soak the green gram for 2-3 hours, strain and set aside.

2   Peel the cucumber, seed and dice into small bits. This should amount to half a cup.

3   In a wok, heat 2 tsps oil for the 1st tempering. Pop the mustard and then add the cumin. Switch off the flame and add the red chillies. As they turn bright red, stir in the green chillies, curry leaves and asafoetida.

4   Grind this tempering along with the soaked gram, coconut, coriander leaves and garlic into a paste, neither coarse nor fine.

5   Add the lemon juice and salt.

6   Squeeze out water from the chopped cucumber and stir the cucumber into the pachchadi.

7   Heat the remaining oil for the 2nd tempering. Pop the mustard and then add the cumin. Switch off the flame and add the curry leaves. Garnish the pachchadi with this crunchy tempering.

Serve with steamed rice and a dollop of ghee.

VARIATIONS

1. Substitute coconut with raw mango.

2. Alternately, reduce the quantity of coconut to ¼ cup and add ¼ cup grated raw mango.

RAW MANGO CHUTNEY *Māmidikāya Pachchadi*

an ingenious combination of sour mangoes, jaggery and chillies

Sour raw mangoes *3*
Jaggery or sugar *1½ tsps*
Oil *3 tbsps*
Salt *to taste*

The 1st tempering
Split black gram (husked) *1½ tbsps*
Mustard seeds *1½ tbsps*
Fenugreek seeds *8-10*
Red chillies *20, nicked at tail with stalks retained (Too spicy? Okay, 15 - relents Pedatha)*
Green chillies *2-4, whole with stalks removed*
Curry leaves *8-10, with stem*
Coriander leaves *2-3 tbsps, chopped roughly*
Asafoetida powder or paste *½ tsp*

The 2nd tempering
Mustard seeds *½ tsp*
Fenugreek seeds *¼ tsp*

1 Wash and pat dry the mangoes. Peel, grate and set aside.

2 In a wok, heat 2½ tbsps oil for the 1st tempering. Add the gram; as it turns golden, add the mustard and then the fenugreek. Switch off the flame and with the browning of the fenugreek, add the red chillies. As they turn bright red, stir in the remaining ingredients of the 1st tempering along with the jaggery.

3 Grind this tempering into a coarse paste without adding any water. Now add the grated mangoes and salt and grind coarsely.

4 Heat the remaining oil for the 2nd tempering. Pop the mustard and then add the fenugreek. As the fenugreek turns brown, switch off the flame. Garnish the pachchadi with this crunchy tempering.

Traditionally eaten with steamed rice and a dollop of ghee, this pachchadi also tastes good as a spread on toast or as an accompaniment to idlis and dosas.

CHUTNEY WITH SOUR GREENS (ROZELLE) *Gōngoora Pachchadi*  *pic. p. 18*

one of the most popular pachchadis of Andhra cuisine

Gōngoora leaves, red stemmed *1 bunch*
Oil *1 cup*
Salt *to taste*

The 1st tempering
Mustard seeds *2 tsps*
Fenugreek seeds *½ tsp*
Red chillies *10-12, nicked at tail with stalks retained*
Green chillies *3-4, whole with stalks removed*
Curry leaves *10-12, with stem*
Coriander leaves *½ cup, chopped roughly*
Asafoetida powder or paste *1 tsp*

The 2nd tempering
Mustard seeds *1 tsp*
Fenugreek seeds *½ tsp*
Red chillies *2-3, nicked at tail with stalks retained*
Asafoetida powder or paste *¼ tsp*
Garlic (optional) *6-8 flakes*

1   Chop the gōngoora leaves along with the tender stems. This should amount to about 6 cups.

2   Heat ¾ cup oil in a wok and add the gōngoora leaves. Cook well for 20-25 minutes on a low flame, stirring occasionally. This leaf has a strange cooking temperament. As soon as it starts cooking, it shrinks and gets pasty thereby misleading the novice into thinking that it is done. But patience! says Pedatha. Continue until the oil separates from the leaves and the water evaporates completely. Once cooked, the gōngoora shrinks to less than a cup. Set aside.

3   In another wok, heat 2 tbsps oil for the 1st tempering. Pop the mustard and add the fenugreek. Switch off the flame and with the browning of the fenugreek, add the red chillies. As they turn bright red, stir in the remaining ingredients of the 1st tempering.

4   Grind this tempering and salt into a coarse paste. Do not add water while grinding. Now add the cooked gōngoora and grind coarsely. It must retain a certain stringy quality.

5   Heat the remaining oil for the 2nd tempering. Pop the mustard and then add the fenugreek. Lower the flame and with the browning of the fenugreek, add the garlic and red chillies. As the chillies turn bright red, add the asafoetida. Garnish the pachchadi with this tempering.

Serve with steamed rice and a dollop of ghee.

Pedatha says...
If you wish to preserve the pachchadi for a longer period, avoid the green chillies and add a few more red chillies instead.

RIPE RED CHILLY PICKLE *Korivikāram*

made during summer months when naturally ripened red chillies are available

Fresh ripe red chillies *¼ kg*
Thick tamarind pulp *1 tbsp*
Oil *4 tbsps*
Salt *to taste*

The 1st tempering
Split black gram (husked) *1 tbsp*
Mustard seeds *1 tsp*
Fenugreek seeds *¼ tsp*
Asafoetida powder or paste *1 tsp*
Coriander leaves *1 tbsp, chopped roughly*

The 2nd tempering
Mustard seeds *½ tsp*
Fenugreek seeds *½ tsp*
Asafoetida powder or paste *¼ tsp*

1 In a wok, heat 2 tbsps oil and on a low flame, fry the chillies for 2-3 minutes. To ensure even frying, do few chillies at a time, remove from oil and place on absorbent paper. Set aside.

2 Heat 1½ tbsps oil for the 1st tempering. Add the gram; as it turns golden, pop the mustard and then add the fenugreek. Switch off the flame and with the browning of the fenugreek, add the asafoetida and coriander leaves.

3 Grind this tempering along with the tamarind pulp and salt into a fine paste. Now add the fried chillies and grind coarsely.

4 Heat the remaining oil for the 2nd tempering. Pop the mustard and then add the fenugreek. Switch off the flame and with the browning of the fenugreek, add the asafoetida and stir for a few seconds. Add this tempering to the pickle.

5 Store in a clean airtight bottle. Can be preserved for months.

Serve with idlis, dosas or a meal, or simply mix into steamed rice with a dollop of ghee.

GRATED MANGO PICKLE *Māmidikāya Thokku*

an all time favourite

Raw mangoes *4*
Mustard powder *2 tbsps*
Chilly powder *3 tbsps*
Turmeric powder *1 tsp*
Jaggery *½ cup*
Oil *½ cup*
Salt *to taste*

The tempering
Mustard seeds *1 heaped tbsp*
Fenugreek seeds *1 tbsp*
Asafoetida powder or paste *½ tsp*

Pedatha says...
Make this delicious pickle using 2 very sour mangoes and 2 not so sour ones; rumani and malgova are good varieties to use.

1   Wash and pat dry the mangoes. Grate along with skin. If the skin is too thick, you can peel it off.

2   Heat the oil in a wok, pop the mustard and then add the fenugreek. Lower the flame and with the browning of the fenugreek, add the asafoetida.

3   Add the grated raw mangoes and remaining ingredients. Roast for 12-15 minutes or until the oil separates. Switch off the flame and set aside to cool.

4   Store this pickle in a clean airtight bottle in the refrigerator.

Serve with steamed rice and a dollop of ghee, or as an accompaniment to a meal.

Anticlockwise from top left:
Gōngoora Pachchadi **p. 15**
Theeya Dhōsakāya Pulusu Pachchadi **p. 7**
Pesarapappu Pachchadi **p. 13**
Pālakoora Pachchadi **p. 3**

CHUTNEYS *Pachchadi*

POWDERS *Podi*

RICE *Annam*

VEGETABLES *Koora*

DALS *Pappu, Chāru*

YOGURT *Perugu*

SWEETS *Theepi*

CRISPIES *Vadiyālu*

A typical Andhra meal would be incomplete without an array of interesting podis to choose from. Made with different grams and spices, each has its own unique flavour and usage. Mixed into steamed rice with a dollop of ghee/oil or served as an accompaniment to idlis and dosais, these powders have made Andhra cuisine famous.

There are two types of podis: the first five in this collection - Kandhi podi, Nuvvulu podi, Podi chutney, Karivēpāku podi and Kothimeeri podi - are mixed into rice and eaten. The last four - Koora podi, Vāngi bāth podi, Sāmbār podi and Chāru podi - are used in the cooking of many dishes.

We enjoyed rice and podi when mixed by Pedatha, but saw stars when we tried the same at home. Much later we realised that it was that dollop of ghee that made all the difference. No wonder she looked so distraught every time we spoke cholesterol - conscious words.

SESAME SEED POWDER *Nuvvulu Podi*  pic. p. 30

a delicious podi with the goodness of sesame

Oil *1 tbsp*
Salt *to taste*

To be roasted without oil
Sesame seeds *200 gms*
Split black gram (husked) *1 tbsp*
Bengal gram *1 tbsp*
Coriander seeds *1 tbsp*
Asafoetida powder *1 tsp*

To be roasted in oil
Red chillies *2 cups, stalks removed*
Curry leaves *¼ cup*

Serve with idlis, dosas or mix into steamed rice with a dollop of ghee or sesame oil.

Pedatha says...

Enhance the flavour of vegetables like broad beans, raw banana or cluster beans by adding this powder as a seasoning, refer p. 46.

1   Dry roast the sesame, grams and coriander seeds, each separately on a low flame, to deep brown.

2   Dry roast the asafoetida powder for a few seconds.

3   Heat the oil and roast the chillies on a low flame until crisp and bright red, but not brown. Remove the chillies from the oil and set aside. Now, roast the curry leaves until crisp and dark green. Remove from oil and set aside.

4   Grind all these ingredients along with salt into a powder, neither too fine nor too coarse. Refer to Pedatha's tip (p. 82) for the correct method of powdering sesame. Cool and store in an airtight container.

POWDERED CHUTNEY *Podi Chutney*

Andhra's popular podi - spicy and tasty

Oil *4 tbsps*
Ghee *2-3 tsps*
Salt *to taste*

To be roasted without oil
Bengal gram *1 cup*
Split black gram (husked) *1 cup*
Poppy seeds *1 tbsp*
Dry coconut *¾ cup, grated*

To be roasted in oil
Red chillies *2 cups, stalks removed*
Curry leaves *½ cup, without stems*
Asafoetida *small marble-sized chunk*
Tamarind *large lemon-sized*

The tempering
Split black gram (husked) *1 tbsp*
Mustard seeds *1 tsp*
Asafoetida powder *1 tsp*

1   On a low flame, dry roast the grams, each separately, to a deep brown.

2   Dry roast the poppy seeds and dry coconut, each separately, to golden brown.

3   Heat 3 tbsps oil and roast the chillies until crisp and bright red, but not brown. Remove the chillies from the oil and set aside. Now, roast the curry leaves until crisp and dark green. Remove from oil and set aside.

4   In the same oil, roast the asafoetida (after tearing it into bits) for 10-15 seconds. Press with a ladle so it roasts well. Remove from oil and set aside. Alternately, you may dry roast 1 tsp of readymade asafoetida powder.

5   Next, roast the tamarind. Press with the ladle so it roasts well. Remove from oil and set aside.

6   Grind all these ingredients along with salt into a coarse powder.

7   Heat the remaining oil for tempering. Add the gram; as it turns golden, pop the mustard and switch off the flame. Add the asafoetida and pour this tempering into the prepared powder and mix well with your fingers.

8   Finally, pour in warm ghee and mix well. Cool and store in an airtight container.

This mouth watering (or should we say, eye watering!) podi mixed with steaming rice makes a great 'lazy day' meal. Serve with idlis and dosas too.

Pedatha says...

If you are not accustomed to handling spices with your fingers, it can be quite a fiery experience. Feel free to use a spoon.

CURRY LEAF POWDER *Karivēpāku Podi*

a nutritious powder made with fresh tender curry leaves

Jaggery or sugar (optional) *1 tbsp*
Oil *4 tbsps*
Salt *to taste*

To be roasted without oil
Split black gram (husked) *2 tsps*
Bengal gram *2 tsps*

To be roasted in oil
Curry leaves *2 cups*
Red chillies *10-12, stalks removed*
Asafoetida powder *small marble-sized chunk*
Tamarind *medium lemon-sized*

7   Grind all these ingredients along with salt and jaggery into a powder, neither too fine nor too coarse. Cool and store in an airtight container.

Serve with idlis, dosas or mix into steamed rice.

Pedatha says...
For a sharp variation, roast 2-3 tbsps grated ginger in ½ tsp ghee for 2-3 minutes. Grind along with the powder.

1   Wash the curry leaves and pat dry.

2   Dry roast the grams, each separately on a low flame, to deep brown.

3   Heat the oil and roast the curry leaves on a low flame until crisp. Take care to see that they remain green. Remove from oil and set aside.

4   In the same oil, roast the chillies until crisp and bright red, but not brown. Remove the chillies from the oil and set aside.

5   Next, roast the asafoetida (after tearing it into bits) for 10-15 seconds. Press with a ladle so it roasts well. Remove from oil and set aside. Alternately, you may dry roast 1 tsp of readymade asafoetida powder.

6   Finally, roast the tamarind. Press with the ladle so it roasts well. Remove from oil and set aside.

CORIANDER LEAF POWDER *Kothimeeri Podi*

the ever-refreshing flavour of coriander is preserved in this powder

Oil *4 tbsps*
Salt *to taste*

To be roasted without oil
Split black gram (husked) *2 tsps*
Bengal gram *2 tsps*

To be roasted in oil
Coriander leaves *2 cups*
Red chillies *10-12, stalks removed*
Asafoetida *small marble-sized chunk*

The tempering
Mustard seeds *½ tsp*
Fenugreek seeds *¼ tsp*

1   Wash the coriander leaves and pat dry.

2   On a low flame, dry roast the grams, each separately, to deep brown.

3   Heat 3½ tbsps oil and roast the coriander leaves for 2-3 minutes. Take care to see that they remain green. Remove from oil and set aside.

4   In the same oil, roast the chillies on a low flame until crisp and bright red, but not brown. Remove from oil and set aside.

5   Next, roast the asafoetida (after tearing it into bits) for 10-15 seconds. Press with a ladle so it roasts well. Remove from oil and set aside. Alternately, you may dry roast 1 tsp of readymade asafoetida powder.

6   Grind all these ingredients along with salt into a powder, neither too fine nor too coarse.

7   Heat the remaining oil for tempering. Pop the mustard and then add the fenugreek. As the fenugreek turns brown, mix this tempering into the powder. Cool and store in an airtight container.

Serve with idlis, dosas or mix into steamed rice with a dollop of ghee or sesame oil.

RED GRAM POWDER *Kandhi Podi*

a popular, lip-smacking podi

Oil *1 tbsp*
Salt *to taste*

To be roasted without oil
Split red gram *1 cup*
Bengal gram *1½ cups*
Roasted gram *1½ cups (this is lighter than bengal gram in colour, readily available in Indian stores)*
Cumin seeds *¾ tbsp*

To be roasted in oil
Red chillies *2 heaped cups, stalks removed*
Curry leaves *½ cup*
Asafoetida *small marble-sized chunk*

Serve with steamed rice and a dollop of ghee or sesame oil.

1   On a low flame, dry roast the grams and cumin, each separately - the roasted gram to a light brown, the others to deep brown.

2   Heat the oil and roast the chillies on a low flame until crisp and bright red, but not brown. Remove the chillies from the oil and set aside. Now, roast the curry leaves until crisp and dark green. Remove from oil and set aside.

3   In the same oil, roast the asafoetida (after tearing it into bits) for 10-15 seconds. Press with a ladle so it roasts well. Remove from oil and set aside. Alternately, you may dry roast 1 tsp of readymade asafoetida powder.

4   Grind all these ingredients along with salt into a powder, neither too fine nor coarse. Cool and store in an airtight container.

BRINJAL RICE POWDER *Vāngi Bāth Podi* *pic. p. 30*

an exotic cooking podi, with a unique combination of spices

Oil *2 tsps*
Ghee *2 tbsps*
No salt required

To be roasted dry
Coriander seeds *1¼ cups*

To be roasted in oil
Red chillies *2 cups, stalks removed*

To be roasted in ghee
Nāgasāgarālu *1 cup*
Kallupāchi *1 cup*
Marātimoggu *½ cup*
Anāspuvvu *½ cup*
Cardamom *½ tbsp*
Cloves *½ tbsp*
Nutmeg *½ tbsp*
Mace *3 stalks*

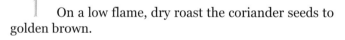

1   On a low flame, dry roast the coriander seeds to golden brown.

2   Heat the oil and roast the chillies on a low flame until crisp and bright red, but not brown. Remove from oil and set aside.

3   Roast the remaining ingredients in ghee until their aromas rise. But here's the catch! Every ingredient has to be roasted separately, using just enough ghee for each.

4   Finally, grind the ingredients of steps 1, 2 & 3 (this time ALL together) into a fine powder. Cool and store in an airtight container.

Apart from Vāngi Bāth, this powder adds a special flavour to vegetable preparations or in Sāmbār also.

Nāgasāgarālu *also known as Nāgkesar, looks like cloves.*

Kallupāchi *black and white, looks like burnt crumbled paper.*

Marātimoggu *black in colour, looks like small thick stems.*

Anāspuvvu *also known as Star anise, brown in colour, resembles a tiny star.*

Recipe using Vāngi Bāth Podi: Vāngi Bāth (p. 34)

Pedatha says...

This powder is well worth the effort because it can be stored for years in an airtight container without refrigeration.

CURRY POWDER *Koora Podi* *pic. p. 30*

enhance the taste of vegetables with this powder

Oil *2 tbsps*
No salt required

To be roasted without oil
Bengal gram *1 cup*
Split black gram (husked) *1 cup*
Dry coconut *¼ cup, grated*

To be roasted in oil
Red chillies *1 cup, stalks removed*
Curry leaves *½ cup*
Asafoetida *small marble-sized chunk*

1   On a low flame, dry roast the grams, each separately, to deep brown. Roast the dry coconut without oil until golden brown.

2   Heat the oil and roast the chillies on a low flame until crisp and bright red, but not brown. Remove from oil and set aside. Now, roast the curry leaves until crisp and dark green. Remove from oil and set aside.

3   In the same oil, roast the asafoetida (after tearing it into bits) for 10-15 seconds. Press with a ladle so it roasts well. Remove from oil and set aside.

4   Grind all these ingredients into a fine powder. Cool and store in an airtight container.

Some tips on how to use Koora Podi:

1. RIDGE GOURD VEGETABLE
   Beerakāya Koora
   Peel ridge gourd and dice into medium-sized pieces. Heat the oil and temper with split black gram (husked), mustard seeds, chillies, curry leaves and asafoetida powder.
   Add chopped onions and turmeric powder and cook for 2-3 minutes. Add the ridge gourd. Cover and cook for 2 minutes. Add koora podi, salt and some water and cook till the vegetable is done. You may add a dash of roasted and powdered sesame seeds in the end.

2. The same recipe can be followed using snake gourd or boiled potato.

3. BITTER GOURD VEGETABLE
   Kākarakāya Koora
   Boil chopped bitter gourd along with turmeric powder. Strain. Follow the above ridge gourd recipe.
   Make a powder of roasted gram and roasted sesame seeds. Mix this into the vegetable with a little jaggery and cook for 2 minutes. Switch off the flame and add a dash of lemon juice.

4. STUFFED BITTER GOURDS
   Kākarakāya Koorina Koora
   Scrape and slit the bitter gourds partially. Remove the seeds. Make a mixture of chopped onions, ginger, garlic, coriander leaves, koora podi and salt. Stuff the bitter gourds with this mixture carefully. Roast in oil until bitter gourds are well cooked.

SAMBAR POWDER *Sāmbār Podi*

a must in every South Indian kitchen

Oil *½ tsp*
No salt required

To be roasted without oil
Coriander seeds *1 cup*
Fenugreek seeds *1 tbsp*
Dry coconut *¼ cup, grated*

To be roasted in oil
Red chillies *20-25, stalks removed*

Recipes using *Sāmbār Podi:*
Sāmbār (p. 58) and *Theeyati*
Pulusu (p. 60)

1   On a low flame, dry roast the coriander and fenugreek, each separately, until deep brown. Roast the dry coconut without oil until golden.

2   Heat the oil and roast the chillies on a low flame until crisp and bright red. Remove from oil and set aside.

3   Grind all these ingredients into a fine powder. Cool and store in an airtight container.

This powder can be used in making any Sāmbār, also adds a distinctive flavour to vegetables.

RASAM POWDER *Chāru Podi*

a must for an aromatic rasam

Oil *2 tsps*
Ghee *½ tsp*
No salt required

To be roasted dry
Coriander seeds *1 cup*
Fenugreek seeds *1¼ tbsps*
Cumin seeds *½ cup*

To be roasted in oil
Red chillies *10-12, stalks removed*
Curry leaves *15-20, stems removed*
Asafoetida *small marble-sized chunk*

To be roasted in ghee
Peppercorns *1½ tbsps*

4   Heat the ghee and roast the peppercorns until the aroma rises. Remove from ghee and set aside.

5   Grind all the ingredients into a fine powder. Cool and store in an airtight container.

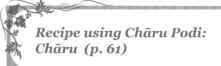

Recipe using Chāru Podi:
Chāru (p. 61)

1   On a low flame, dry roast the coriander, fenugreek and cumin, each separately, until deep brown.

2   Heat the oil and roast the chillies until crisp and bright red, but not brown. Remove the chillies from the oil and set aside. Now, roast the curry leaves until crisp and dark green. Remove from oil and set aside.

3   In the same oil, roast the asafoetida (after tearing it into bits) for 10-15 seconds. Press with a ladle so it roasts well. Remove from oil and set aside.

Anticlockwise from top left:
Vāngi Bāth Podi **p. 26**
Nuvvulu Podi **p. 21**
Koora Podi **p. 27**

CHUTNEYS *Pachchadi*

POWDERS *Podi*

RICE *Annam*

VEGETABLES *Koora*

DALS *Pappu, Chāru*

YOGURT *Perugu*

SWEETS *Theepi*

CRISPIES *Vadiyālu*

Although Andhra cuisine is famous for its spread of pachchadis and podis as accompaniments to its staple fluffy, white steamed rice, there are also some specialty rice dishes. A sure success, these recipes are well worth their time and effort.

Pedatha's *Vāngi bāth* is the family's absolute favourite, while her Bisi bele huli has never seen leftovers. Both these recipes are a clear indication of the Karnataka influence in her cooking.

Pulihōrā is the most popular rice preparation of this cuisine, both in everyday cooking and during celebrations.

Ponni or Nellore varieties of rice are preferred in most South Indian homes for day-to-day cooking. But of course, on special occasions, one does indulge in Basmati.

SPICY DAL AND VEGETABLE RICE *Bisi Bele Huli*   *pic. p. 38*

a delicious combination of rice and vegetables

Uncooked rice *1 heaped cup*
Split red gram *1 level cup*
Turmeric powder *½ tsp*
Onion *1 large*
Potato *1 medium*
Carrot *1 medium*
French beans *7-8*
Thick tamarind pulp *3 tbsps*
Green chillies *2, slit*
Curry leaves *10-12, with stems*
Ghee *4-6 tbsps*
Oil *2-3 tbsps*
Salt *to taste*

The 1st powder
Bengal gram *½ cup*
Split black gram (husked) *¼ cup*
Coriander seeds *¼ cup*
Red chillies *6-7, nicked at tail with stalks retained*
Cinnamon *3 sticks, each 1½ inches long*
Cloves *4*

The 2nd powder
Dry coconut *½ cup, grated*
Coriander leaves *¼ cup*

The tempering
Mustard seeds *1 tsp*
Fenugreek seeds *½ tsp*
Asafoetida powder *½ tsp*

1   Pressure-cook the rice in 3 cups of water until soft, but not pasty. Set aside.

2   Pressure-cook the gram in 3 cups of water along with turmeric powder to a very soft consistency. Churn well and set aside.

3   Chop the vegetables into medium-sized bits.

4   For the 1st powder, dry roast the grams and coriander seeds, each separately, on a low flame until deep brown. Heat 2 tsps oil and roast the chillies until crisp and bright red. Do not roast the cinnamon and cloves. Grind all these ingredients into a fine powder and set aside.

5   For the 2nd powder, wash the coriander leaves and pat dry. Roast the dry coconut without oil until golden brown. Grind along with coriander leaves coarsely, without adding any water. Set aside.

6   In a large wok, heat the remaining oil for tempering. Pop the mustard and then add the fenugreek. Lower the flame and with the browning of the fenugreek, add the asafoetida and chopped vegetables.

7   Cover and cook until the vegetables are done. Add ½ cup water if required.

8   Make a smooth gravy of the tamarind pulp, the 1st powder and the cooked gram in 1 cup water. Add this to the vegetables and cook for 2-3 minutes. Keep stirring to avoid lumps.

9   Add the cooked rice, green chillies, curry leaves and salt and continue to stir for another five minutes.

10   Finally, just before switching off the flame, stir in the 2nd powder and ghee.

Serve hot with Aratidhoota Perugu Pachchadi (p. 67) and some Vadiyālu from the crispies section.

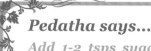

Pedatha says...
Add 1-2 tsps sugar in step 8 and enjoy the difference.

BRINJAL RICE *Vāngi Bāth* pic. p. 38

the most exotic and closest-to-the-heart dish in this collection, tastes excellent even without brinjals

Uncooked rice *1 cup*
Turmeric powder *¼ tsp*
Vāngi bāth podi (p. 26) *1 level tbsp*
Brinjals *4-5, medium-sized, quartered*
Potato *1 large, diced medium*
Capsicum *1, diced medium*
Green peas *½ cup, shelled and boiled*
Ghee *4-6 tbsps*
Oil *4-6 tbsps*
Salt *to taste*

The powder
Split black gram (husked) *¼ cup*
Bengal gram *¼ cup*

The paste
Dry coconut *¼ cup, grated*
Green chillies *1-2, whole with stalks removed*
Coriander leaves *½ bunch*

The tempering
Split black gram (husked) *1½ tsps*
Mustard seeds *1 tsp*
Green chillies *3-4, whole with stalks removed*
Asafoetida powder *1 tsp*
Curry leaves *1 stem*

2   For the powder, dry roast the grams on a low flame until they turn golden in color. Grind into a fine powder and set aside.

3   For the paste, roast the dry coconut without oil until golden. Grind with the green chillies and coriander leaves, using very little water.

4   To the cooled rice, add half the paste, the Vāngi bāth podi and salt. Add ghee and mix gently.

5   Heat the oil for tempering. Add the gram, as it turns golden, pop the mustard. Lower the flame and add the other ingredients of the tempering.

6   Add the chopped vegetables; stir and cook well without adding any water.

7   Add the peas, remaining paste and prepared powder. Cook for a couple of minutes on low flame.

8   Finally, add the seasoned rice, mix well and switch off the flame.

Serve hot with Theeya Dhōsakāya Perugu Pachchadi (variation on p. 67) and some Vadiyālu from the crispies section.

1   Boil the rice with the turmeric powder. Each grain of the cooked rice must be separate but soft. Strain and cool.

TANGY TAMARIND RICE *Pulihōrā* pic. p. 38

**a perfect travel-time dish, this delicious rice stays fresh for up to
two days, and what's better - needs no reheating**

Uncooked rice *2 cups*
Tamarind pulp *1 cup, thick but not pasty*
Turmeric powder *½ tsp*
Fenugreek seeds *½ tsp*
Sesame seeds *3-4 tbsps*
Roasted peanuts *¼ cup*
Asafoetida powder *¼ tsp*
Ghee *1 tbsp*
Oil *2½ tbsps*
Salt *to taste*

The 1st tempering
Bengal gram *1 tbsp*
Split black gram (husked) *1 tbsp*
Mustard seeds *1 tbsp*
Red chillies *5-6, halved*
Green chillies *2-3, slit*
Curry leaves *10-12*

The 2nd tempering
Bengal gram *1 heaped tsp*
Split black gram (husked) *1 tsp*
Mustard seeds *½ tsp*
Green chillies *2-3, slit*
Curry leaves *10-12*

1   Boil the rice with the turmeric powder. Each grain of the cooked rice must be separate but soft. Strain and cool.

2   Roast the fenugreek, grind into a fine powder.

3   Roast the sesame seeds on a low flame until golden and grind to a coarse powder. Refer to Pedatha's tip (p. 82) for the correct method of powdering sesame.

4   Heat 1½ tbsps oil for the first tempering. Add the grams, and as they turn golden, pop the mustard. Lower the flame and add the other ingredients of the tempering.

5   Add the tamarind pulp and simmer for 3-4 minutes. Add the asafoetida, fenugreek and sesame powders and simmer for a couple of minutes.

6   Add the cooled rice and salt, mix well and switch off the flame.

7   Heat the remaining oil for the second tempering. Add the grams, and as they turn light golden, pop the mustard. Add the peanuts and roast until light brown. Switch off the flame and add the green chillies, curry leaves and ghee.

8   Garnish the tamarind rice lavishly with this crunchy tempering.

Serve with some Vadiyālu from the crispies section.

Pedatha says...

1. A tbsp of koora podi (p. 27) along with the powdered sesame adds a special flavour to this dish.

2. Since it is difficult to grind just ½ tsp of fenugreek, you may grind a larger quantity and preserve. When we asked Pedatha whether one could grind the fenugreek along with sesame, she explained that if the sesame is ground too fine, it would let out oil and get pasty.

RAW MANGO RICE *Māmidikāya Annam*

a lip-smacking experience with rice and raw mango

Uncooked rice *2 cups*
Sour raw mango *2, medium*
Turmeric powder *½ tsp*
Oil *3 tbsps*
Salt *to taste*

The paste
Mustard seeds *1 tsp*
Fresh coconut *½ cup, grated*
Green chillies *2-4, whole with stalks removed*
Coriander leaves *1 tbsp*

The tempering
Bengal gram *1½ tsps*
Split black gram (husked) *2 heaped tsps*
Mustard seeds *1 tsp*
Red chillies *3-4, nicked at tail with stalks retained*
Asafoetida powder *¼ tsp*
Curry leaves *10-12*
Roasted peanuts *2 tbsps*

1 Boil the rice with the turmeric powder. Each grain of the cooked rice must be separate but soft. Strain and cool.

2 Wash, peel and grate the mangoes. Set aside.

3 Grind the ingredients for the paste to a fine consistency, using very little water.

4 Heat the oil for tempering. Add the grams, and as they turn golden, pop the mustard. Lower the flame and add the other ingredients of the tempering.

5 Add the grated mangoes and stir for 2-3 minutes. Add the paste and stir for a minute.

6 Finally, add the cooled rice and salt, mix well and switch off the flame.

Serve hot with some Vadiyālu from the crispies section.

CURD (YOGURT) RICE *Dhadhyōdhanam*

the last course in an Andhra meal, with a special dash of mustard paste

Uncooked rice *1 heaped cup*
Yogurt *2 cups*
Creamy milk *½ cup, boiled and cooled*
Pomegranate or green grapes *for garnishing*
Oil *1 tsp*
Salt *to taste*

The paste
Mustard *¼ tsp*
Green chillies *2-3*
Coriander leaves *1 sprig*

The tempering
Split black gram (husked) *1 heaped tsp*
Mustard seeds *1 tsp*
Asafoetida powder *½ tsp*

1 Pressure-cook the rice in 3 cups of water until pasty.

2 Using a ladle, mash the cooked rice a little while still hot. Cool and stir in the milk gently. Ensure that no lumps remain.

3 For the paste, soak the mustard in 1 tbsp water for 10 minutes. Grind along with the chillies and coriander.

4 Stir this paste and salt into the yogurt and mix well with the rice.

5 Heat the oil and add the gram. As the gram turns golden, pop the mustard and then add the asafoetida. Switch off the flame and add this tempering to the yogurt-rice.

6 Decorate lightly with pomegranate or halved green grapes.

Serve with fried Majjiga Mirapakāya (p. 81)

> ### Pedatha says...
> *1. Add a generous dollop of cream, removed from the top of cooled milk, for a creamier and tastier flavour.*
>
> *2. For a simpler and quicker recipe, omit the paste, and simply chop the green chillies and coriander leaves and add to the yogurt-rice.*

Clockwise from top left:
Bisi Bele Huli **p. 33**
Pulihōrā **p. 35**
Vāngi Bāth **p. 34**

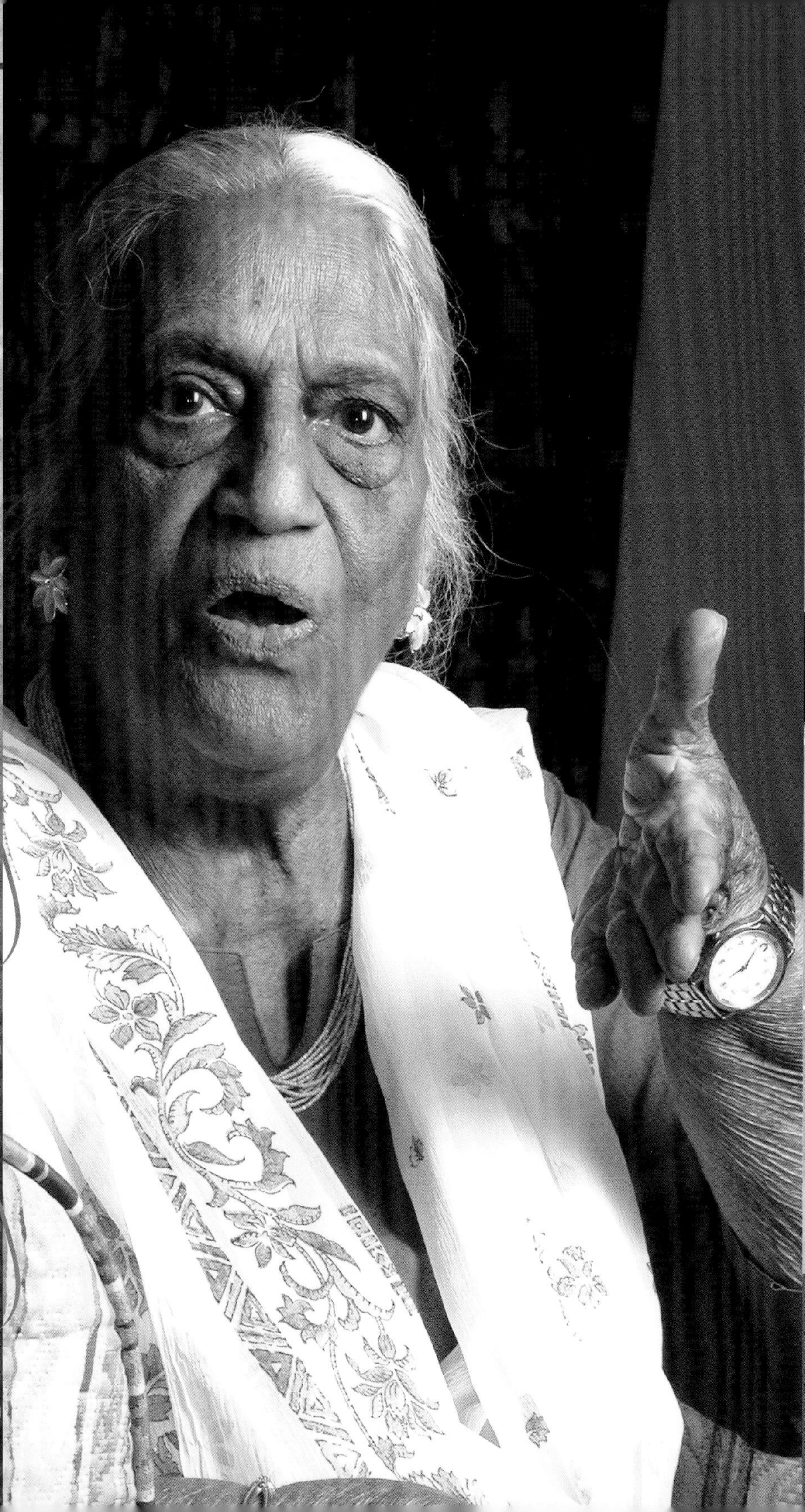

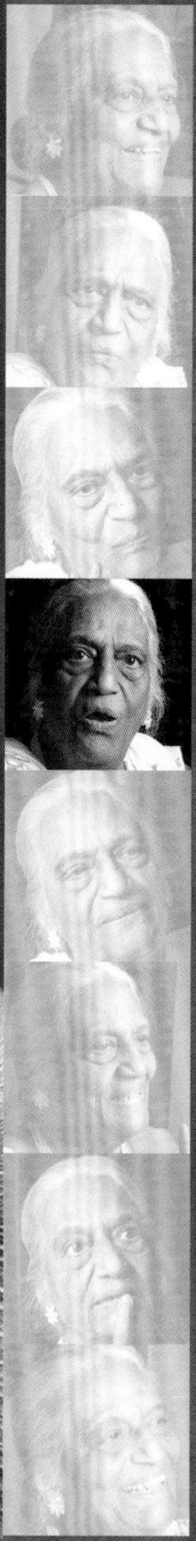

Simple or exotic, these delicious side-dishes to an Andhra meal are characterized by Pedatha's special touch. Some of them are wholesome enough to be a complete meal when eaten with rice.

To cook with Pedatha, some preliminaries are a must: excitement, lots of patience and of course, a few podis, always at hand. Her favourites are Koora podi, Nuvvulu podi, and even sesame, just roasted and powdered. They lend a special touch to the simplest of vegetable preparations.

Naturally, all vegetables should be washed well before cooking, but Pedatha says take greater care with greens as they tend to be gritty.

"An ingenious solution I had for my youngest son's dislike for vegetables was to pack them in containers from my sister Subhadra's (a.k.a. Pedatha's) house, and watch with a mixture of jealousy and satisfaction while he polished them off under the mistaken impression that she had made them. I am told that this is practiced quite successfully even today by all of Subhadra's grandchildren, nephews, and nieces."

Mrs. Sarla Surya Rao

LEAFY VEGETABLE *Thōtakoora Koora*

a unique combination of greens and roasted gram

Amaranth leaves *2 bunches*
Roasted gram *2-3 tbsps, powdered*
Oil *1 tbsp*
Salt *to taste*

The paste
Ginger *1 inch piece*
Garlic *2 flakes*
Coriander leaves *½ cup*
Green chillies *4*

The tempering
Split black gram (husked) *1 tsp*
Mustard seeds *2 tsps*
Turmeric powder *¼ tsp*
Asafoetida powder *1 tsp*
Curry leaves *6-7, with stem*

1 Chop the greens roughly along with the tender stems. This should amount to about 6 cups after chopping.

2 Grind the ingredients for the paste using a little water.

3 In a wok, heat the oil for tempering. Add the gram; as it turn golden, pop the mustard. Lower the flame and add the turmeric, asafoetida and curry leaves.

4 Add the greens and stir. Cover and cook until well done.

5 Now, add the paste and salt and continue to cook for 2-3 minutes.

6 Finally, switch off the flame and stir in the powdered gram.

Serve with steamed rice or as a side dish in a meal.

VARIATION
You may substitute the amaranth with spinach.

FRESH FENUGREEK VEGETABLE *Menthi Koora*

a delight for fenugreek lovers

Fenugreek leaves *2 large bunches*
Split red gram *½ cup*
Asafoetida powder or paste *1 tsp*
Wheat flour *1 tbsp*
Green chillies *2, slit*
Jaggery or sugar (optional) *2 tsps*
Coconut *2 tbsps, grated*
Coriander leaves *½ cup, chopped fine*
Ghee *1 tbsp*
Oil *1 tbsp*
Salt *to taste*

The tempering
Split black gram (husked) *1 tbsp*
Mustard seeds *1 tbsp*
Red chillies *5-7, nicked at tail*
Curry leaves *a few*

1 Chop the fenugreek along with the tender stems. This should amount to about 4 cups after chopping.

2 Boil the red gram in a pan of water until the gram is well-cooked but remains whole. Strain the water and use the same in some other preparation if you like.

3 Dry roast the wheat flour until its aroma rises. Add the sugar and set aside.

4 In a wok, heat the oil for tempering. Add the gram; as it turns golden, add the mustard. Lower the flame and add the red chillies.

5 As they turn bright red, stir in the curry leaves and the fenugreek leaves. Cover and cook until well done.

6 Add the cooked gram, roasted wheat flour, green chillies, asafoetida and salt. Stir and cook for a while.

7 Finally, pour in the ghee just before switching off the flame. Garnish with the grated coconut and coriander leaves.

Serve with steamed rice or as a side dish in a meal.

BANANA STEM VEGETABLE *Aratidhoota Koora*

a simple side-dish made special with a dash of sesame

Banana stem *2 cups, chopped (refer step 1)*
Turmeric powder *½ tsp*
Sesame seeds *2 tbsps*
Oil *2 tbsps*
Salt *to taste*

The tempering
Split black gram (husked) *2 tsps*
Mustard seeds *1 tsp*
Red chillies *3-4, nicked at tail with stalks retained*
Green chillies *2, slit*
Curry leaves *a few*
Asafoetida powder *¼ tsp*

Serve with steamed rice and any pappu from this collection.

Pedatha says...

Banana stem is very good for those suffering from kidney stones and gall bladder disorders.

VARIATION

WITH RIDGE GOURD OR SNAKE GOURD
Scrape the skin and chop the vegetable into ½ inch cubes. Follow the recipe from step 3.

1   Discard the outer layer of the banana stem. Chop stem into thick round slices. As you chop, discard the fibrous strands and soak in buttermilk or water to avoid discolouration. Wash well and dice into small bits.

2   Boil the chopped vegetable in water with turmeric powder until done. Strain and set aside.

3   Roast the sesame seeds on a low flame until golden and grind to a coarse powder. Refer to Pedatha's tip (p. 82) for the correct method of powdering sesame.

4   In a wok, heat the oil for tempering. Add the gram; as it turns golden, add the mustard. Lower the flame and add the red chillies. As they turn bright red, stir in the green chillies, curry leaves and asafoetida.

5   Add the vegetable and salt. Cook for 5-6 minutes.

6   Finally, add the powdered sesame just before switching off the flame.

POTATO WITH GREENS *Bangāladhumpa Koora*

a healthy combination of potatoes and greens

Potatoes *2*
Amaranth leaves (or Spinach) *2 bunches*
Turmeric powder *¼ tsp*
Oil *2 tbsps*
Salt *to taste*

The paste
Coconut *3 tbsps, grated*
Green chillies *2, whole with stalks removed*
Roasted gram *3 tbsps*
Garlic (optional) *5 small flakes*
Ginger *1 inch piece*
Coriander leaves *¼ cup*

The tempering
Split black gram (husked) *1 tsp*
Mustard seeds *½ tsp*
Red chillies *3-4, nicked at tail*
Curry leaves *a few*
Asafoetida powder *1 level tsp*

1   Chop greens roughly along with the tender stems. This should amount to about 6 cups.

2   Parboil the potatoes, peel and dice into medium-sized pieces.

3   Grind the ingredients for the paste using a little water.

4   In a wok, heat the oil for tempering. Add the gram; as it turns golden, add the mustard. Lower the flame and add the red chillies. As they turn bright red, stir in the curry leaves and asafoetida powder.

5   Add the greens, potatoes and turmeric powder. Cover and cook until the potatoes are fully done.

6   Finally, add the paste and salt and cook for 5-6 minutes.

Serve with steamed rice and any pappu from this collection.

BRINJAL PASTY VEGETABLE *Vankāya Muddha Koora*

a side-dish with a remarkable combination of brinjal and black-eyed beans

Brinjal *½ kg, chopped medium*
Black-eyed beans *½ cup*
Turmeric powder *1 tsp*
Ginger *1 tsp, grated*
Coriander leaves *1 tbsp, chopped fine*
Green chillies *3-4, slit*
Oil *2 tbsps*
Salt *to taste*

The tempering
Split black gram (husked) *2 tsps*
Mustard seeds *1 tsp*
Red chillies *2-3, nicked at tail with stalks retained*
Curry leaves *8-10, with stem*
Asafoetida powder *1 tsp*

Serve with steamed rice and any pachchadi from this collection.

1   Soak the black-eyed beans in warm water for half an hour and pressure-cook up to one whistle. Strain and set aside.

2   Boil the brinjal with turmeric powder until well cooked. Strain and mash coarsely.

3   In a wok, heat the oil for tempering. Add the gram; as it turns golden, add the mustard. Lower the flame and add the red chillies. As they turn bright red, stir in the curry leaves and asafoetida.

4   Add the mashed brinjal and the boiled beans, green chillies, ginger and salt. Cook for 8-10 minutes.

5   Finally, switch off the flame and garnish with coriander leaves.

BROAD BEANS VEGETABLE *Peddha Chikkudukāya Koora* *pic. p. 50*

always a success

Tender broad beans *½ kg*
Turmeric powder *½ tsp*
Jaggery or sugar (optional) *1 tbsp, powdered*
Sesame seeds *1 tbsp*
Oil *1 tbsp*
Salt *to taste*

The tempering
Split black gram (husked) *1 tsp*
Mustard seeds *1 tsp*
Red chillies *2-3, slit*
Green chillies *2, slit*
Curry leaves *8-10, with stem*
Asafoetida powder *¼ tsp*

The garnish
Coconut *2 tbsps, grated*
Coriander leaves *2 tbsps*
Green chillies *2*

Serve as an accompaniment to a meal.

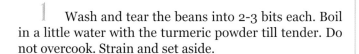

1   Wash and tear the beans into 2-3 bits each. Boil in a little water with the turmeric powder till tender. Do not overcook. Strain and set aside.

2   Dry roast the sesame seeds on a low flame until golden and grind to a coarse powder. Refer to Pedatha's tip (p. 82) for the correct method of powdering sesame.

3   In a wok, heat the oil for tempering. Add the gram; as it turns golden, add the mustard. Lower the flame and add the chillies, curry leaves and asafoetida.

4   Add the boiled vegetable and cook for 2-3 minutes. Stir in the jaggery, sesame powder and salt.

5   Grind the ingredients for the garnish very coarsely. Better still, pound them with a pestle and mortar, says Pedatha. Add to the vegetable and switch off the flame.

Pedatha says...

If you have 'Nuvvulu Podi' (p. 21) ready at hand, use it instead of the plain powdered sesame.

VARIATION

WITH CLUSTER BEANS OR RAW BANANA
Substitute broad beans with cluster beans or raw banana. Follow the rest of the recipe with a dash of tamarind pulp and crushed ginger along with the jaggery.

MUSTARD FLAVOURED VEGETABLE *Āva Pettina Koora*

raw banana with a twang of mustard

Raw bananas *2, diced medium*
Turmeric powder *¼ tsp*
Oil *1 tbsp*
Salt *to taste*

The paste
Mustard seeds *1½ tsps*
Raw rice *1 tbsp*
Ginger *1 inch piece*
Coconut *¼ cup, grated*
Coriander leaves *¼ cup*

The tempering
Split black gram (husked) *½ tsp*
Mustard seeds *½ tsp*
Green chillies *2-4, slit*
Curry leaves *a few*
Asafoetida powder *a pinch*

VARIATION
You may substitute raw banana with cabbage or sweet pumpkin in the above recipe.

1   Boil the diced bananas in water along with turmeric powder till tender. Strain and set aside.

2   For the paste, soak the mustard and rice in a little water. Grind finely along with the other ingredients of the paste.

3   In a wok, heat the oil for tempering. Add the gram; as it turns golden, add the mustard. Lower the flame and add the green chillies, curry leaves and asafoetida.

4   Add the boiled vegetable, paste and salt. Mix well and continue to cook for 3-4 minutes. Switch off the flame.

Serve as an accompaniment to chapatis or rice.

BEANS WITH STEAMED GRAM *Pātōli*

the famous combination of vegetable with steamed and crumbled gram

French beans *¼ kg, chopped fine*
Turmeric powder *¼ tsp*
Oil *3 tbsps*
Salt *to taste*

The paste
Bengal gram *½ cup*
Split red gram *½ cup*
Pepper corns *¼ tbsp*
Cumin seeds *¼ tbsp*
Green chillies *4-5, whole with stalks removed*
Ginger *2 inch piece*
Coriander leaves *¼ cup*

The tempering
Mustard seeds *1 tsp*
Red chilly *1, halved*
Green chilly *1, slit*
Asafoetida powder *¼ tsp*

1 Boil the beans in water along with turmeric powder and a little salt till tender. Strain and set aside.

2 For the paste, soak the bengal gram and red gram in warm water for 30 minutes. Strain the grams and grind along with the other ingredients of the paste and a little salt. Add just enough of the strained water to grind into a coarse mixture.

3 Steam this mixture for 10-12 minutes in a pressure cooker, without the whistle. Cool, crumble and set aside.

4 In a wok, heat the oil for tempering and pop the mustard. Lower the flame and add the chillies and asafoetida powder.

5 Add the boiled beans and gram mixture. Cover and cook for 5-7 minutes, stirring occasionally. Sprinkle a little of the strained water if the consistency is too dry. Check the seasoning and add salt if required.

6 The ideal consistency of this nutritious pātōli should be light and fluffy.

Serve as an accompaniment to a meal. A great combination with Theeyati Pulusu (p. 60) and steamed rice.

VARIATION
Substitute the french beans with broad beans, capsicum or cluster beans in the above recipe.

BRINJAL ROAST *Vankāya Vēpudu*

an Andhra favourite

Brinjals *½ kg*
Red chilly powder *1 tbsp*
Oil *3-4 tbsps*
Salt *to taste*

The tempering
Split black gram (husked) *1 tsp*
Mustard seeds *½ tsp*
Asafoetida powder *¼ tsp*
Turmeric powder *¼ tsp*
Curry leaves *6-8*

1 Quarter the brinjals.

2 In a wok, heat the oil for tempering. Add the gram; as it turns golden, add the mustard. Lower the flame and add the remaining ingredients for tempering.

3 Add the vegetable, allow to roast on a low flame, stirring now and then.

4 After about 8-10 minutes, when the brinjals have turned light brown, add the salt and chilly powder. Continue cooking on a low flame until well done. If you like your vegetable crunchier, drizzle some more oil while cooking.

Serve as a side dish with a meal.

VARIATIONS

This vepudu can be made with almost any vegetable.

1. POTATO ROAST *pic. facing page*
Bangāladhumpa Vēpudu
Peel and dice 5-6 large potatoes into ½ inch cubes. Follow the recipe.

2. BITTER GOURD ROAST
Kākarakāya Vēpudu
Scrape the skin and chop the bitter gourd into thin rounds. Soak in water with salt, turmeric and a little tamarind paste for 20 minutes. Strain and squeeze out the vegetable to remove some of its bitterness. Wash and set aside. Follow the recipe. Consider adding a dash of jaggery or sugar.

3. LADY'S FINGER ROAST
Bendakāya Vēpudu
Wash, pat dry and chop into rounds. Follow the recipe, but with less oil. You may drizzle some oil once the lady's finger has lost its stickiness.

Clockwise from top left:
Pindimiriyam **p. 59**
Pālakoora Pappu **p. 53**
Peddha Chikkudukāya Koora **p. 46**
Bangāladhumpa Vēpudu (Variation) **p. 49**

This protein packed section consists of the gravy accompaniments to rice. In contrast to the chutneys and powders, many of the dals or 'pappu' as they are called in Telugu, are not as spicy. There are exceptions to the rule, like the Pindimiriyam, which is as peppery as its name suggests. The South Indian Sāmbār, of course, needs no introduction. The section ends with Chāru, popularly known as rasam, a much loved dish of South India.

We have also included Theeyati pulusu which strictly speaking, is a category by itself, neither a dal nor a vegetable. A pulusu is a thick sour gravy used as a 'nanchuko' which when roughly translated means 'to be eaten along with a meal, as a side-dish.'

Unlike in North India where the dal preparation is named after the lentil with which it is cooked, the Andhra pappu is usually named after the greens or vegetable it is cooked along with. For example, Chintha chiguru pappu - Dal with tender tamarind leaves or Aratidhoota pappu - Dal with banana stem.

RED GRAM WITH SPINACH *Pālakoora Pappu*

referred to by its Kannada name 'Hulipalya' in the family, this unusual version of the usual combination of gram and spinach is a finger-licking favourite

Spinach leaves *1 large bunch*
Split red gram *1 cup*
Fenugreek seeds *¼ tsp*
Turmeric powder *½ tsp*
Tamarind pulp *2-3 tbsps*
Asafoetida powder *1 heaped tsp*
Green chillies *3, slit*
Curry leaves *1 stem*
Coriander leaves *½ cup, chopped fine*
Ghee *3 tbsps*
Oil *3 tbsps*
Salt *to taste*

The tempering
Mustard seeds *1 tbsp*
Fenugreek seeds *1 tbsp*
Red chillies *8-10, nicked at tail with stalks retained*

1 Pressure-cook the red gram in 3 cups of water with the fenugreek and ¼ tsp turmeric to a very soft consistency. Churn well and set aside.

2 Chop spinach roughly along with the tender stems. This should amount to about 4 cups after chopping.

3 In a wok, heat the oil for tempering. Pop the mustard and then add the fenugreek. Lower the flame and with the browning of the fenugreek, add the red chillies. As they turn bright red, add the spinach, cover and cook until well done.

4 Add the tamarind pulp, asafoetida and salt and simmer for 5-7 minutes.

5 Add the cooked gram, ¼ tsp turmeric, green chillies, curry leaves and coriander leaves and continue to cook for a few minutes.

6 Finally, just before switching off the flame, add the ghee (3 tbsps! Well, reduce the quantity if you are cholesterol or figure conscious).

Serve with steamed rice and a spicy pachchadi from this collection.

VARIATIONS

WITH OTHER GREENS
Substitute spinach with amaranth in the above recipe.

WITH FENUGREEK LEAVES
Substitute spinach with fenugreek leaves in the recipe. While tempering, omit the fenugreek seeds and add cumin instead.

WITH GREEN GRAM
Substitute red gram with husked green gram, fenugreek with cumin and tamarind with 1-2 tbsps of lemon juice. Add the lemon juice just before switching off the flame.

DAL WITH BANANA STEM *Aratidhoota Pappu*

a tasty dal with the healthy banana stem

Banana stem *1 cup, chopped (refer step 2)*
Split red gram *1 cup*
Turmeric powder *½ tsp*
Tamarind pulp *4 tbsp*
Jaggery (optional) *2-3 tsps*
Oil *2 tbsps*
Salt *to taste*

The tempering
Split black gram (husked) *1 tsp*
Mustard seeds *1 tsp*
Fenugreek seeds *1 tsp*
Red chillies *1-2, nicked at tail with stalks retained*
Curry leaves *7-8, with stem*
Asafoetida powder or paste *1 tsp*

1   Pressure-cook the red gram in 3 cups of water to a very soft consistency. If the cooked gram is too thick, add ½ cup water. Churn well and set aside.

2   Discard the outer layer of the banana stem. Chop stem into thick round slices. As you chop, discard the fibrous strands and soak in buttermilk or water to avoid discolouration. Wash well and dice into small bits.

3   In a wok, heat the oil for tempering. Add the gram; as it turns golden, add the mustard and then the fenugreek. Lower the flame and with the browning of the fenugreek, add the red chillies. As they turn bright red, stir in the curry leaves and asafoetida.

4   Add the chopped banana stem and stir for a minute.

5   Add the turmeric powder, tamarind pulp, jaggery and salt and cook until the vegetable is well done.

6   Finally, add the cooked gram and simmer for a few minutes.

Serve with steamed rice and a spicy pachchadi from this collection.

Pedatha says...
You may substitute red gram with green gram (husked).

GREEN GRAM WITH RIDGE GOURD *Beerakāya Pesarapappu*

a pappu made with healthy green gram

Green gram (husked) *¾ cup*
Ridge gourd *2, medium*
Turmeric powder *¼ tsp*
Green chillies *2, stalks removed & halved*
Coriander leaves *2 tbsps, chopped*
Lemon juice *1 tbsp*
Oil *1 tbsp*
Salt *to taste*

The tempering
Mustard seeds *1 tsp*
Cumin seeds *½ tsp*
Red chillies *2, nicked at tail with stalks retained*
Curry leaves *1 stem*
Asafoetida powder *¼ tsp*

1 Pressure-cook the green gram with turmeric in 3 cups of water to a soft consistency. If the cooked gram is too thick, add ½ cup water. Churn well and set aside.

2 Scrape and chop the gourds into medium-sized cubes.

3 In a wok, heat the oil for tempering and pop the mustard. Lower the flame and add the cumin and red chillies. As the chillies turn bright red, stir in the curry leaves and asafoetida.

4 Add the chopped gourds, cover and simmer for a couple of minutes until tender.

5 Add the cooked gram, green chillies, coriander leaves and salt and continue to cook for a few minutes.

6 Finally, switch off the flame and stir in the lemon juice.

Serve with steamed rice and a spicy pachchadi from this collection. Fried Majjiga Mirapakāya (p. 81) is a great accompaniment.

Pedatha says...

1. For a special touch, add a generous pinch of cumin powder and black pepper powder just before switching off the flame.

2. For an extra special touch, as soon as the tempering is done, add 1 tbsp ghee before adding the vegetables.

VARIATIONS

WITH ANY GOURD
Substitute ridge gourd with snake gourd or bottle gourd in the recipe. Alternately, you may also combine all the three gourds.

Vankāya Māmidi Pesarapappu
Substitute ridge gourd with brinjals and raw mango in the recipe.

DAL WITH TOMATOES *Tamātā Pappu*

an everyday pappu in most Andhra homes

Split red gram *1 cup*
Tomatoes *3-4, chopped fine*
Fenugreek seeds *8-10*
Turmeric powder *¼ tsp*
Garlic (optional) *3-4 flakes, roughly crushed*
Chilly powder *1 tsp*
Coriander powder *1 tsp*
Green chillies *3-4, stalks removed & halved*
Coriander leaves *2 tbsps, chopped*
Oil *1 tbsp*
Salt *to taste*

The tempering
Mustard seeds *1 tsp*
Fenugreek seeds *1 tsp*
Curry leaves *7-8, with stem*
Asafoetida powder or paste *1 tsp*

1   Pressure-cook the red gram in 3 cups of water along with the fenugreek seeds and turmeric to a very soft consistency. If the cooked gram is too thick, add ½ cup water. Churn well and set aside.

2   In a wok, heat the oil for tempering. Pop the mustard and then add the fenugreek. Lower the flame and with the browning of the fenugreek, add the curry leaves and asafoetida.

3   Add the chopped tomatoes and garlic, stir and simmer for a few minutes.

4   Add chilly powder, coriander powder, green chillies and salt and cook for a few minutes or until the tomatoes turn pasty. Now add the cooked gram and allow to simmer for 2-3 minutes.

5   Just before switching off the flame, add the coriander leaves.

Serve with steamed rice and a spicy pachchadi from this collection.

Pedatha says...

For a special touch, add 1 tbsp ghee and a few slices of raw mango just before adding the tomatoes to the tempering.

DAL WITH TENDER TAMARIND LEAVES *Chintha Chiguru Pappu*

choose fresh tender tamarind leaves for this tasty pappu

Tamarind leaves *1 cup*
Split red gram *1 cup*
Brinjals *2-3, quartered*
Turmeric powder *¼ tsp*
Oil *2 tbsps*
Salt *to taste*

The tempering
Mustard seeds *1 tsp*
Fenugreek seeds *1 tsp*
Red chillies *1-2, halved*
Curry leaves *1 stem*
Asafoetida powder *¾ tsp*

VARIATIONS

Māmidi Chiguru Pappu
Add one sour raw mango in the above recipe for a tangier variation.

Māmidikāya Pappu
You can also make this pappu only with raw mango; without any brinjal or tamarind leaf. The raw mango will take 10-15 minutes to cook. Add a dash of jaggery in the end.

1   Chop the tamarind leaves finely or crush between your palms.

2   Pressure-cook the red gram in 3 cups of water with the turmeric powder to a soft consistency. Churn well and set aside.

3   In a wok, heat the oil for tempering. Pop the mustard and then add the fenugreek. Lower the flame and with the browning of the fenugreek, add the red chillies. As they turn bright red, stir in the curry leaves and asafoetida powder.

4   Add the tamarind leaves and chopped brinjals. Cover and simmer. After 2-3 minutes, add a cup of water. Continue to simmer until the vegetables are well done.

5   Finally, add the salt and cooked gram and simmer for a few minutes.

Serve with steamed rice and a spicy pachchadi from this collection.

SAMBAR WITH VEGETABLES *Sāmbār*

this dal preparation popular in all of South India needs no introduction

Split red gram *1 cup*
Fenugreek seeds *8-10*
Turmeric powder *¼ tsp*
Baby onions *½ cup, peeled*
Tomato (optional) *1, chopped medium*
Any vegetable (refer tip) *1 cup, chopped medium*
Tamarind pulp *2 tbsps*
Sāmbār podi (p. 28) *1-2 tbsps*
Green chillies *3-4, slit*
Coriander leaves *2 tbsps, chopped roughly*
Jaggery (optional) *1-2 tsps*
Oil *1 tbsp*
Salt *to taste*

The tempering
Mustard seeds *½ tsp*
Fenugreek seeds *½ tsp*
Curry leaves *10-12, with stem*
Asafoetida powder or paste *1 tsp*

Serve hot with idlis, dosas or steamed rice and a dollop of ghee.

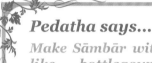

Pedatha says...
Make Sāmbār with any vegetable like bottlegourd, drumstick, pumpkin, lady's finger, carrot or radish, or a combination of the above.

1 Pressure-cook the red gram in 3 cups of water with the fenugreek and turmeric to a soft consistency. If the cooked gram is too thick, add ½ cup water. Churn well and set aside.

2 In a thick bottomed vessel, heat the oil for tempering. Pop the mustard and then add the fenugreek. Lower the flame and with the browning of the fenugreek, add the curry leaves and asafoetida.

3 Add the onions, tomatoes and vegetable. Sprinkle water, cover and simmer until well done.

4 Add the tamarind pulp and cook for a couple of minutes. Then add sāmbār podi, cooked gram and salt and continue to simmer for a while.

5 Finally, add the jaggery, green chillies and coriander leaves and switch off the flame.

PEPPER FLAVOURED DAL WITH VEGETABLES *Pindimiriyam*

pic. p. 50

for those who grew up in an Andhra home, this will bring back forgotten flavours

Split red gram *¾ cup*
Turmeric powder *¼ tsp*
Bottle-gourd *4-6 cubes, medium-sized*
Potato *1 large, diced medium*
Raw banana *1, diced medium*
Brinjals *2-3, quartered*
Beans *10-12, chopped into 2 inch pieces*
Cluster beans *½ cup, chopped into 2 inch pieces*
Coriander leaves *¼ cup, chopped fine*
Tamarind pulp *1½ tbsps*
Oil *5 tbsps*
Salt *to taste*

The paste
Split black gram (husked) *¾ tbsp*
Cumin seeds *½ tbsp*
Coriander seeds *2 heaped tbsps*
Peppercorns *1 tbsp*
Red chillies *5-6, whole with stalks retained*
Coconut *½ cup, grated*

The tempering
Mustard seeds *2 tsps*
Cumin seeds *2 tsps*
Curry leaves *10-12 leaves, with stem*
Asafoetida powder or paste *½ tsp*

1   Boil the vegetables in a little water with turmeric until tender. Set aside along with water.

2   Pressure-cook the red gram in 2½ cups of water to a soft consistency. Churn well and set aside. If too thick, mix a little water from the vegetables.

3   For the paste, heat 3 tbsps oil in a wok and add the black gram. As the gram turns golden, lower the flame and add the remaining ingredients for the paste except the coconut. Roast for a couple of minutes. Now, add the coconut and continue to roast for a minute. Grind into a fine paste, using very little water.

4   In the same wok, heat the remaining oil for tempering. Pop the mustard and add the cumin. Lower the flame and add the curry leaves and asafoetida powder.

5   Add the prepared paste and allow to simmer for a few minutes. Add the boiled vegetables, tamarind pulp, chopped coriander leaves and salt. Simmer for 3-5 minutes.

6   Finally, stir in the cooked gram and simmer for 4-5 minutes, allowing the flavours to blend well.

Serve hot with steamed rice.

Pedatha says...
Add a special touch to this pepper flavoured recipe by pouring in 2 tbsps of ghee just before switching off the flame.

VARIATION
WITH BITTER GOURD
Substitute this combination of vegetables with ½ kg bitter gourd chopped into rounds. However, do not use any water from the boiled vegetable as it will be bitter.

VEGETABLES IN A SWEET AND SOUR GRAVY *Theeyati Pulusu*

a festive recipe, always made in large quantities - this recipe serves 6-8

Pumpkin (red) *100 gms*
Bottle gourd *100 gms*
Sweet potato *100 gms*
Brinjal *100 gms*
Raw mango *100 gms*
Drumsticks *2*
Tamarind pulp *3 tbsps*
Sāmbār podi (p. 28) *2 tbsps*
Jaggery *1½ tbsps*
Green chillies *3-4, slit*
Curry leaves *8-10, with stem*
Coriander leaves *for garnishing*
Oil *2 tbsps*
Salt *to taste*

The powder
Split black gram (husked) *1 tbsp*
Bengal gram *1 tbsp*
Sesame seeds *1 tsp*

The tempering
Mustard seeds *1 tsp*
Fenugreek seeds *1 tsp*
Asafoetida powder *¾ tsp*

1   Cut vegetables into large chunks, retaining the skin of all except bottle-gourd and sweet potato.

2   For the powder, dry roast the grams and sesame until deep brown and grind to a fine consistency.

3   Mix this powder, tamarind pulp, sāmbār podi and jaggery in 1-1½ cups of water to make a thin, smooth gravy.

4   In a wok, heat the oil for tempering. Pop the mustard and then add the fenugreek. Lower the flame and with the browning of the fenugreek, add the asafoetida powder.

5   Add the chopped vegetables and allow to simmer, adding enough water to cover the vegetables.

6   When the vegetables are well done, add the prepared gravy, green chillies and salt and cook for 4-5 minutes.

7   Finally, garnish with curry leaves and coriander leaves just as you switch off the flame.

Serve as a side dish with steamed rice and any pappu from this collection. You can also add cluster beans and raw banana to this recipe.

RASAM *Chāru*

also known as 'Pappu Chāru', this is the popular South Indian soup

Water *5-6 cups*
Split red gram *¼ cup*
Tomatoes *2 large, quartered*
Tamarind pulp *3-4 tbsps*
Chāru podi (p. 29) *1 tbsp*
Asafoetida powder or paste *1 tsp*
Curry leaves *10-12, with stem*
Coriander leaves *2 tbsps, chopped roughly*
Ghee *2 tsps*
Salt *to taste*

The tempering
Mustard seeds *½ tsp*
Fenugreek seeds *½ tsp*
Cumin seeds *½ tsp*

1   Pressure-cook the red gram in 1 cup of water. Churn and set aside.

2   In a deep vessel, heat 1 tsp of ghee for tempering. Pop the mustard and then add the fenugreek. Lower the flame and with the browning of the fenugreek, add the cumin.

3   Add the tomatoes, tamarind pulp, chāru podi, salt and 5 cups of water. Bring to a boil.

4   Mash the tomatoes lightly with a ladle and add the cooked gram. Allow to boil for 4-5 minutes.

5   Just before switching off the flame, add asafoetida, curry leaves and coriander leaves.

6   Finally, pour in the remaining ghee.

Serve hot with steamed rice or enjoy as a soup.

SWEET RASAM *Theeyati Chāru*

a nourishing variation of Chāru using powdered gram instead of the usual boiled gram

Water *5-6 cups*
Split red gram *1 tbsp*
Tamarind *medium lemon-sized, to be used whole*
Turmeric powder *½ tsp*
Jaggery or sugar *1-2 tbsps*
Ginger *2 inch piece, crushed*
Garlic *5-6 cloves, crushed*
Coriander seeds *½ tbsp, roasted and powdered*
Peppercorns *½ tbsp, roasted and powdered*
Cumin seeds *½ tbsp, roasted and powdered*
Coriander leaves *to garnish*
Ghee *1 tbsp*
Salt *to taste*

The tempering
Mustard seeds *½ tsp*
Cumin seeds *½ tsp*
Asafoetida powder *½ tsp*

Pedatha says...

Add a small stick of cinnamon and a tsp of Chāru Podi (p. 29) for added flavour. This Chāru is very good for constipation and digestive problems.

1   Wipe the red gram with a damp cloth and grind into a fine powder.

2   Measure 5-6 cups of water in a deep vessel and add all the ingredients except the tempering, coriander leaves and ghee and bring to a boil. Allow to simmer for 10 minutes.

3   Heat the ghee and pop the mustard. Add the cumin and asafoetida and pour this tempering into the chāru. Garnish with coriander leaves.

Serve hot with steamed rice or enjoy as a soup.

CHUTNEYS *Pachchadi*

POWDERS *Podi*

RICE *Annam*

VEGETABLES *Koora*

DALS *Pappu, Chāru*

YOGURT *Perugu*

SWEETS *Theepi*

CRISPIES *Vadiyālu*

Recipes using yogurt (perugu) or buttermilk (majjiga) can be found in every state of India. When cooked with a combination of spices and vegetables, they can be very appetizing indeed. The last course of an Andhra meal, like most other Indian meals ends with yogurt to balance out all the indulgences of spices and oil.

It is said in folklore that buttermilk is like a mother for one who has no mother...it soothes, it nourishes, it nurtures. Try the Menthi majjiga as a cooling drink after a spicy meal or on hot summer days.

"Talk of nurturing and the person I think of is Subhadra Dodamma (a.k.a. Pedatha). We have never been able to count the number of dishes she has served to family and friends, let alone the number of dishes she knows. Each time the women in the family thought they had the full list, she would come up with a dozen more, each of whose histories dated back not less than five or six decades."

P. Sainath
Magsaysay Awardee 2007 for Journalism,
Literature & Creative Communication

A GRAVY WITH YOGURT *Majjiga Pulusu*

a tasty and wholesome gravy with steamed rice

Thick sour yogurt *2 cups*
Drumsticks *2, chopped into 3 inch pieces*
Pumpkin (white) *5-7 cubes, medium-sized*
Oil *2-3 tsps*
Salt *to taste*

The paste
Mustard seeds *¼ to ½ tsp*
Bengal gram *½ cup*
Cumin seeds *½ tsp*
Asafoetida powder *¼ tsp*
Fresh coconut *½ cup, grated*
Ginger *2 inch piece*
Green chillies *3-4*
Coriander leaves *¼ cup*
Curry leaves *5-7*

The tempering
Fenugreek seeds *½ tsp*
Mustard seeds *½ tsp*
Cumin seeds *1 tsp*
Green chillies *2, slit*
Curry leaves *10-12, with stem*

1   Churn yogurt with 2 cups water and set aside.

2   Boil the vegetables in just enough water until tender. Set aside along with the water.

3   For the paste, soak the mustard and bengal gram in a little warm water for 15-20 minutes. Grind along with the rest of the ingredients of the paste to a fine consistency and mix into the yogurt.

4   Heat the oil in a wok for tempering. Pop the mustard and then add the fenugreek. As the fenugreek turns brown, lower the flame and stir in the other ingredients of the tempering.

5   Add the vegetables and yogurt mixture. Boil for 5-6 minutes on a low flame, stirring continuously.

6   Finally, add salt just before switching off the flame. Garnish with some chopped coriander leaves.

Serve hot with steamed rice.

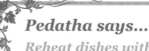

Pedatha says...

Reheat dishes with yogurt on a low flame stirring all the while as the yogurt may tend to curdle.

VARIATION

Substitute the vegetables in the above recipe with bottle gourd and chow-chow.

GREENS IN YOGURT *Ākukoora Majjiga Pulusu*

known as 'Thonthana' in the family, this is an unusual and tasty dish from rural Andhra Pradesh

Split red gram *½ cup*
Bengal gram *½ cup*
Amaranth leaves *1 bunch, chopped fine*
Thick yogurt *3 cups, churned*
Tamarind pulp *1 tbsp*
Turmeric powder *½ tsp*
Asafoetida powder *1 tsp*
Green chillies *3, slit*
Curry leaves *1 stem*
Coriander leaves *½ cup, chopped fine*
Ghee *2-3 tbsps*
Oil *3 tbsps*
Salt *to taste*

The paste
Fresh coconut *½ cup, grated*
Ginger *2 inch piece*
Coriander leaves *¼ cup, chopped*
Green chillies *3-4*

The tempering
Mustard seeds *1 tbsp*
Red chillies *6-8, nicked at tail with stalks retained*

1   Cook both the grams together in 3 cups of water to a very soft consistency. Add ½ cup of water, churn well and set aside.

2   For the paste, grind the ingredients to a fine consistency, using a little water. Mix this paste into the cooked grams and set aside.

3   In a wok, heat the oil and pop the mustard. Lower the flame and add the red chillies.

4   As they turn bright red, add the chopped greens. Cover and simmer for 12-15 minutes or until well done, stirring now and then.

5   Add the tamarind, turmeric, asafoetida and salt and simmer for a few minutes.

6   Add the gram mixture, green chillies, curry leaves and coriander leaves and continue to cook for a couple of minutes.

7   Finally, switch off the flame and stir in the ghee and yogurt.

Serve with steamed rice.

VARIATION
Substitute amaranth with spinach in the above recipe.

BANANA STEM IN SPICED YOGURT *Aratidhoota Perugu Pachchadi*

the healthy banana stem in a different avataar

Banana stem ½ cup, chopped (refer step 2)
Turmeric powder ¼ tsp
Thick yogurt 2 cups
Oil 2 tsps
Salt to taste

The paste
Fresh coconut 1-2 tbsps, grated
Mustard seeds ½ tsp
Green chillies 1-2, whole with stalks removed
Ginger 1 inch piece
Coriander leaves 2 tsps, chopped
Asafoetida powder or paste ½ tsp

The tempering
Split black gram (husked) ¾ tsp
Mustard seeds ¾ tsp

Serve as an accompaniment to a meal. A tasty combination with Bisi Bele Huli (p. 33)

VARIATIONS

RED PUMPKIN IN SPICED YOGURT
Erra Gummadikāya Perugu Pachchadi
Substitute banana stem with red pumpkin and follow the same recipe.

CUCUMBER IN SPICED YOGURT
Theeya Dhōsakāya Perugu Pachchadi
Substitute banana stem with cucumber. Do not boil the cucumber, instead add the diced cucumber directly into the yogurt paste.

1   For the paste, soak the mustard in a little water for half an hour. Strain and grind along with the other ingredients of the paste to a fine consistency.

2   Discard the outer layer of the banana stem. Chop stem into thick round slices. As you chop, discard the fibrous strands and soak in buttermilk or water to avoid discolouration. Wash well and dice into small bits.

3   Boil in water with the turmeric powder for 2-3 minutes. Make sure the vegetable doesn't get too soft. Strain and set aside.

4   In a bowl, churn the yogurt and add the paste, cooked vegetable and salt.

5   In a wok, heat the oil for tempering. Add the gram; as it turns golden, pop the mustard. Garnish the yogurt mixture with this crunchy tempering.

FENUGREEK FLAVOURED BUTTERMILK *Menthi Majjiga*

an unusual soothing drink for warm afternoons

Thick yogurt *3 cups, not too sour*
Pepper powder *½ tsp, freshly ground*
Cumin powder *½ tsp, freshly ground*
Oil *2 tsps*
Salt *to taste*

The tempering
Mustard seeds *¼ tsp*
Carom seeds *1 tsp*
Fenugreek seeds *1 level tsp*
Cumin seeds *¼ tsp*
Asafoetida powder *a pinch*
Turmeric powder *a pinch*
Green chillies *2-4, slit*
Curry leaves *1-2 stems*
Coriander leaves *2 tsps, chopped fine*

Pedatha says...

Add ½ tsp ghee to the tempering just before adding it to the buttermilk for a richer flavour.

1   Churn the yogurt with 1½ cups of water to make a thick buttermilk. Add salt and the freshly ground pepper and cumin powders and set aside.

2   In a wok, heat the oil for tempering. Pop the mustard and add the carom and fenugreek. Lower the flame and with the browning of the fenugreek, add the cumin and asafoetida.

3   Switch off the flame and add the remaining ingredients of the tempering.

4   Pour this tempering into the buttermilk.

Serve chilled as an anytime drink. Tastes delicious when mixed with rice.

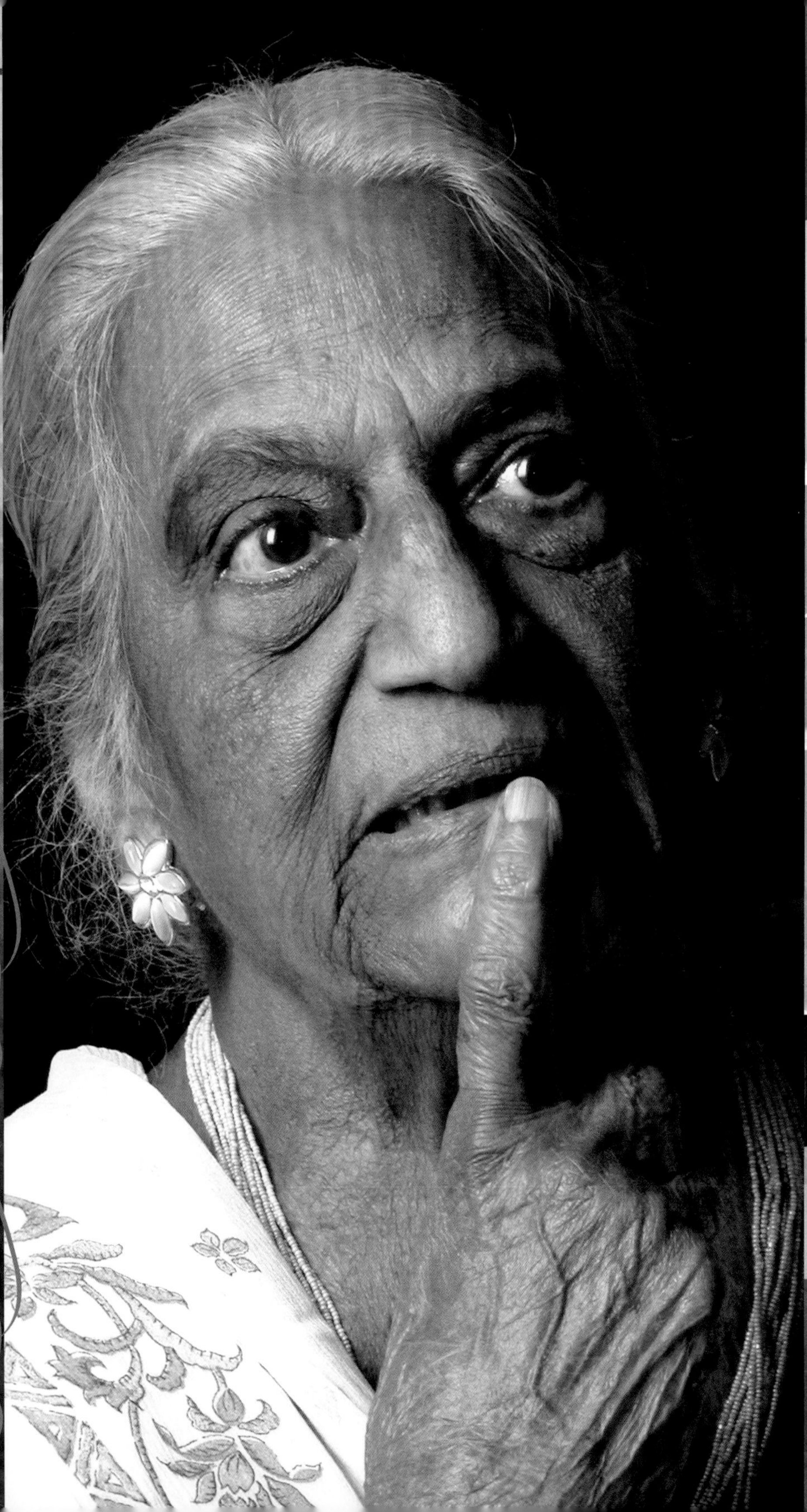

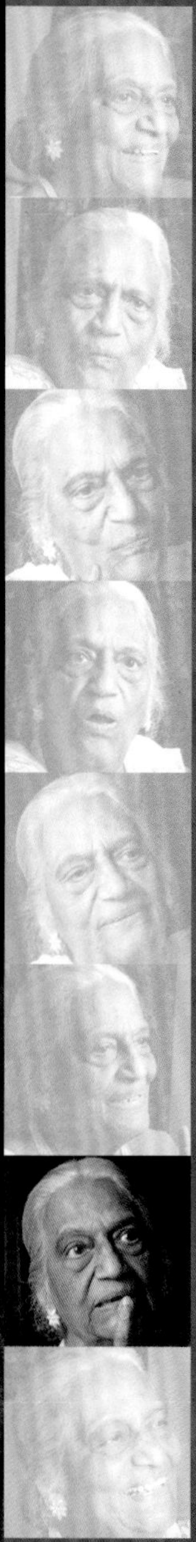

ar from the eye-watering chillies, here are some delicious sweets to complement a meal.

These are recipes that Pedatha, more a lover of chillies rather than sugar or jaggery, does not indulge in too often. In fact, the standing joke in the family is that she would happily cook an entire meal for an army, but for dessert, pack the children off to the nearby sweet shop. But jokes apart, this section carries some of her favourite sweets which she enjoys making.

Pedatha says that as you start enjoying the flavours of saffron and cardamom, you may brave teaspoon measurements rather than small pinches in your desserts.

"Cooking for an army - that's my sister-in-law Subhadra (a.k.a. Pedatha). I remember those times when she hosted many important meetings of the 'All Indian Women's Conference', Delhi. She was a cheerful and enthusiastic host, and used to serve an array of delicacies - Bisi bele huli, Vāngi bāth, Idlis, Pachchadis, Pāyasams, to name a few - each one made to perfection."

Padmabhushan Dr. V. Mohini Giri

SWEET PANCAKES *Bobbatlu*

wholesome and delicious - this dish requires patience and a little practice

The filling
Bengal gram *1 cup*
Sugar *1¼ cups*
Cardamom powder *1 tsp*
Nutmeg powder *½ tsp*

The dough
Plain flour (Maida) *1½ cups*
Sesame oil *1-1½ cups*
Ghee *for roasting the bobbatlu*
Banana leaf *1*

For the filling

1   Pressure-cook the gram with 2 cups of water until soft and pasty. Add the sugar and transfer to a wok. Cook on low flame stirring continuously until it becomes a thick paste and starts to leave the sides of the wok.

2   Add the cardamom and nutmeg powders. Stir and switch off the flame. Set aside to cool.

3   Divide this mixture into 8-10 portions and make into balls.

For the dough

4   Sift the plain flour and knead well with warm water to make a soft dough.

5   Pour the oil in a bowl and soak the dough in the oil for 3-4 hours.

6   Remove the dough from the oil. Allow the oil to drip out of the dough completely.

7   Divide the dough into 8-10 portions and make into balls.

To make the Bobbatlu

8   Wash and pat dry the banana leaf. Coat it with a little ghee.

9   Place a ball of dough on it and pat it flat on the leaf with your palm or fingers.

10   Place a ball of filling in the centre of the dough and seal the edges over it with your fingers.

11   Roll into a 6-7 inch diameter circle. The bobbatlu should be a little thick.

12   Cook on a hot tawa (griddle) on both sides using a little ghee until light brown spots appear.

13   Repeat with the rest of the dough and filling.

Spread ghee or white butter on one side and serve hot.

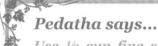

Pedatha says...
Use ½ cup fine semolina (chiroti ravva in the Indian market) along with one cup plain flour for an extra special Bobbatlu. For the health conscious, substitute plain flour with whole wheat flour.

EXOTIC ALMOND DESSERT *Bādām Pāyasam*

a favourite Indian dessert with the richness of almonds

Almonds *20-25*
Milk *1 litre*
Sugar *¾ cup*
Saffron *a pinch*
Cooking camphor *a very small pinch*
Cardamom powder *a pinch*
Pistachios *for decorating, slivered*

Pedatha says...

The camphor adds an interesting flavour to the pāyasam, although it is an acquired taste. Use a very miniscule amount as it can make the pāyasam bitter.

1   Blanch, peel and grind the almonds into a coarse paste. Mix into half the quantity of milk (unboiled) and set aside.

2   Pour the remaining milk in a thick bottomed vessel and bring to a boil. Add the sugar and simmer for 5-7 minutes.

3   Gently pour in the milk with the almond paste, stirring continuously until it comes to a boil.

4   Mix the camphor and saffron in 1 tbsp of warm milk and rub until the milk turns orange. Pour into the pāyasam just before taking off the flame.

5   Add the cardamom powder and decorate with pistachio slivers.

Serve hot or chilled.

MILK AND GRAM DESSERT *Pesarapappu Pāyasam*

a tasty drink with the goodness of green gram and milk

Green gram (husked) *¾ cup*
Raw rice *1 tbsp*
Milk *1 litre*
Thick coconut milk *1 cup*
Jaggery *9-10, 1 inch cubes*
Cooking camphor *a pinch*
Saffron *a pinch*
Cardamom powder *a pinch*
Cashewnuts *2 tbsps*
Raisins *10-12*
Pistachios *for decorating, slivered*
Ghee *1 tsp*

1 Dry roast the gram and rice on a low flame until the aroma rises. Wash well and pressure-cook with 1½ cups of water until well cooked and pasty. Churn well and set aside.

2 Bring the milk to a boil and allow to simmer on a low flame for 10-15 minutes. Set aside.

3 Boil the jaggery in just enough water to cover it. Switch off the flame as soon as the jaggery has melted. Strain to remove any scum.

4 In a thick bottomed vessel, mix the jaggery syrup into the cooked gram. Simmer on a low flame, stirring continuously so that the gram does not stick to the bottom. Bring to a boil and switch off the flame. Allow it to stand for 10-5 minutes. Now slowly stir in the boiled milk and the coconut milk.

5 Mix the camphor and saffron in 1 tbsp of warm milk and rub until the milk turns orange. Pour into the pāyasam.

6 In a wok, heat the ghee and fry the cashews until light golden. Add the raisins, when they puff up, add to the pāyasam. Garnish with pistachio slivers and cardamom powder.

Serve hot or chilled.

Pedatha says...

If the jaggery is not fresh or of good quality, it could cause the milk to curdle. So if you are unsure, substitute jaggery with 1 - 1¼ cups sugar.

SEMOLINA COCONUT BALLS *Kobbarikāya Ravva Laddu*

the mixture of coconut and semolina lends an intriguing texture

Semolina *1 cup*
Fresh coconut *2 cups, grated*
Sugar *1½ cups*
Cashewnuts *8-10, broken into bits*
Raisins *8-10*
Saffron *a pinch*
Cardamom powder *a pinch or two*
Ghee *1 cup*

1 Dry roast the semolina for a minute or two on low flame.

2 Mix with the grated coconut and set aside for 1-2 hours.

3 Heat 1 tbsp ghee and fry the cashews until golden. Remove the cashews and in the same ghee, fry the raisins until they puff up. Set aside.

4 Prepare the saffron by rubbing it in 1 tsp warm milk until the milk turns orange. Set aside.

5 Add little more than ¼ cup of water to the sugar and bring to a boil. Strain to remove scum. Boil again for a couple of minutes. When the syrup starts bubbling, switch off the flame and set aside.

6 In a wok, heat the ghee and roast the semolina-coconut mixture on a low flame for 5-7 minutes or until the mixture turns very light pink.

7 Switch off the flame and add this mixture to the sugar syrup. Add the cashews, raisins, cardamom powder and prepared saffron.

8 When the mixture has cooled a little, make large lemon-sized balls with your palms. The delicious laddus are ready.

Cool and store in an air-tight container.

SEMOLINA FUDGE *Ravva Kēsari*

a popular dish throughout India

Semolina *1 cup*
Sugar *1¼ cups*
Water *2¼ cups*
Cashewnuts *8-10, broken into bits*
Raisins *8-10*
Saffron *a pinch*
Cardamom powder *a pinch or two*
Cooking camphor *a pinch*
Ghee *¼ cup*

Pedatha says...

1. For a tastier, creamier version, you can add 2½ cups boiling milk instead of water.

2. Add a little extra sugar and allow the fudge to cook a little longer. When it becomes sticky, spread evenly on a greased plate. Cool and cut into squares for an interesting variation and neater finish.

1   Dry roast the semolina for 2-3 minutes on low flame.

2   In a pan, heat the water and bring to a boil.

3   Prepare the saffron by rubbing it in 1 tsp warm milk until the milk turns orange. Set aside.

4   Heat the ghee and fry the cashews until golden. Remove the cashews and set aside.

5   In the same ghee, add the raisins. As soon as they puff up, add the semolina and roast for 1-2 minutes. Now, add the sugar and boiling water and allow to cook on a low flame, stirring continuously to avoid lumps. Within minutes, this mixture will become a thick fudge.

6   Add the saffron liquid, fried cashews, cardamom powder and cooking camphor and let it simmer for a minute or two. Switch off the flame as soon as the mixture starts leaving the sides of the pan.

Serve hot or cold.

GRAM BALLS *Minapasunni*

made in a jiffy

Black gram (husked) *2 cups*
Powdered sugar *¾ cup*
Cashewnuts *6-7, broken into bits*
Raisins *8-10*
Cardamom powder *a pinch or two*
Ghee *½ - ¾ cup, as needed*

1   Dry roast the gram until golden brown and grind into a very fine powder.

2   Add the sugar and cardamom powder and mix well.

3   Heat 1 tbsp ghee and fry the cashews until golden. Remove the cashews and in the same ghee, fry the raisins until they puff up. Add the cashews and raisins to the gram mixture.

4   Melt the remaining ghee and pour into the gram mixture slowly. Add enough ghee to bind the mixture for making lemon-sized balls with your palms. The delicious laddus are ready.

Cool and store in an air-tight container.

CHUTNEYS *Pachchadi*

POWDERS *Podi*

RICE *Annam*

VEGETABLES *Koora*

DALS *Pappu, Chāru*

YOGURT *Perugu*

SWEETS *Theepi*

CRISPIES *Vadiyālu*

No Indian meal is complete without the crunch of poppadams and vadiyālu. Dozens of readymade varieties specific to each region are available in all Indian grocery stores. Sunny summer terraces with sheets of drying vadiyālu, a sight that conjures up childhood memories for many of us, is something rarely found in urban apartments these days.

Most vadiyālu need a few days of searing mid-summer heat in order to dry fully. Do not forget to bring the sheet indoors at sundown everyday. If left outdoors, nocturnal insects or rodents could tamper with it or the morning dew could dampen the vadiyālu.

In these days of cholesterol - consciousness, poppadams and vadiyālu are often roasted or microwaved rather than deep fried. But Pedatha will not hear of such a thing. "Everything can be enjoyed if eaten in moderation", she states.

PUMPKIN CRISPIES *Gummadikāya Vadiyālu*

You might need a few tries before you get it right. Always prepare step 1 & 2 the previous evening.

Pumpkin (white) *8-9 cups, diced (refer step 1)*
Split black gram (husked) *½ cup*
Fresh chillies (green or red) *5-7*
Asafoetida paste or powder *1 tsp*
Salt *to taste*

1 Peel the pumpkin, seed and dice into ¼ inch cubes. Add enough salt for the pumpkin.

2 Tie the diced pumpkin in a thin cloth and wring out all the water. Now, leave this overnight pressed under a heavy stone to strain out any remaining water.

3 Soak the gram for 1 hour. Grind along with the chillies, asafoetida and a little salt. Take special care to see that the paste is thick and soft. It must not be grainy at all. Use very little water for the grinding process. Add the diced pumpkin.

4 Spread a clean, thick plastic sheet or cloth on a sunny verandah and drop lemon-sized quantities of the prepared mixture onto the sheet. Note here that the 'vadiyalu' must have air incorporated in them. Therefore, they must not be pressed down or made into balls, but just lightly dropped.

5 Allow the vadiyālu to dry in hot sunlight for a few days until completely dry and hard. Remember to cover the sheet with a fruit net (or a baby net). Bring the sheet indoors at sundown everyday.

6 Once fully dried, store in an airtight container.

Deep fry as and when required, for that special touch to a meal.

BEATEN RICE CRISPIES *Atukulu Vadiyālu*

crispies with a difference

Beaten rice (thick variety) *3 cups*
Onions *2, chopped fine*
Lady's finger *10-12, chopped fine*
Green chillies *5-7, chopped fine*
Asafoetida paste or powder *1 tsp*
Salt *to taste*

1   Soak the beaten rice in water for 1 hour or until it turns soft.

2   Squeeze out the water and mix in the remaining ingredients with your fingers to make a crumbly dough.

3   Spread a clean, thick plastic sheet or cloth on a sunny verandah and drop lemon-sized quantities of the prepared mixture onto the sheet. Cover the sheet with a net.

4   Allow the vadiyālu to dry in hot sunlight for a few days until completely dry and hard. Bring the sheet indoors at sundown everyday.

5   Once fully dried, store in an airtight container.

Deep fry as and when required, to add crunch to a meal.

Pedatha says...

You can use 3-4 tsps of red chilly powder or flakes instead of green chillies if you prefer.

VARIATION

POPCORN VADIYĀLU
Follow the same recipe using ready made popcorn instead of beaten rice. Omit the lady's finger.

SUN DRIED CHILLIES *Majjiga Mirapakāya*

crunchy and spicy - a tasty accompaniment to curd rice

Green chillies *½ kg*
Asafoetida powder *2 heaped tbsps*
Chilly powder *1-2 tsps*
Sour yogurt *1 cup, churned*
Salt *to taste*

The powder
Cumin seeds *½ cup*
Carom seeds *½ cup*

Deep fry as and when required, as a delightful accompaniment to any meal.

1   Wash and pat dry the green chillies. If you like, make a small slit running halfway down one side of every chilly and set aside.

2   Grind the cumin and carom seeds into a fine powder. Add the asafoetida, chilly powder, salt and just enough water to make a thick paste.

3   Soak the green chillies in this paste and pressure-cook for less than a whistle. Switch off the flame and set aside to cool.

4   Add the yogurt to the spiced chillies and pour into a jar. Let it soak well for 3 days. Shake well twice a day.

5   On the 4th day, remove the chillies from the yogurt and spread on a thick plastic sheet or cloth in hot summer sun. Cover the sheet with a net. Within 2-3 days, the chillies will dry fully. Bring the sheet indoors at sundown everyday.

6   Once fully dried, store in an airtight container.

Chēthi ruchi...that special touch

SESAME Powdering sesame seeds is a tricky affair. The best way is to use a pestle and mortar. If using a blender, grind small quantities at a time for a few seconds. Stop and repeat until the sesame reaches a powdery consistency. Otherwise, the sesame seeds let out oil and become pasty. Since it is difficult to grind small quantities of sesame, you may grind a larger quantity and preserve.

TEMPERING This is a skill to be honed. While tempering, ensure that the black gram turns to what Pedatha calls a 'rose red'; the fenugreek golden brown; and the chillies bright red. Mustard should pop well but never burn, she cautions. Therefore, although in many of the recipes the mustard is popped, in others it is 'added' so that it pops by the time the other ingredients are tempered.

FLAME Never cook on a high flame, says Pedatha all the time. Food is tasty when cooked with lots of patience on a low flame.

OIL Use sesame oil in the pachchadis. For everything else, the oil of your preference.
For serving with steamed rice, heat some oil, add a dash of asafoetida powder, cool and preserve in a bottle. Use as and when required.

ASAFOETIDA Roll the asafoetida block into small marbles if soft, or break into small bits. Roast them in a little hot oil on a low flame, pressing down with a flat ladle to ensure even frying. Powder and store. Pedatha prefers this to readymade powder.
You can also soak the asafoetida blocks in just enough water and store in liquid form in the refrigerator. A teaspoon of this paste can be substituted for a teaspoon of powder.

DALS In dal preparations, once the gram is cooked, check the consistency and add water if necessary to the cooked gram. Churn well and set aside. Avoid adding water at the later stages of cooking.
All dal preparations tend to thicken on

cooling, so are best eaten when freshly cooked. However, if reheated, you may add a little water.

CHILLIES Pedatha always makes a small tear at the tail of the chilly before adding it to the tempering. This is only for the dishes where the chilly doesn't have to be ground. She says that while cooking, the chilly fills up with oil which flavours the dish without letting out the seeds. If you like your food spicy, you can squeeze the chilly over the food. The spicy oil that comes out of it makes it a 'yumm' experience.

TAMARIND Boil the tamarind and extract the pulp. This can then be refrigerated for a few days and used as required.

PERSONAL PREFERENCES
Andhra recipes are by and large spicy. The average palette may find the quantity of chillies used in many of the recipes alarming. Therefore Pedatha advises you to use your discretion. The same applies to jaggery, sugar, oil and ghee. In one of our conversations, she sighed with nostalgia about those good old days when no one squirmed at generous quantities of ghee or oil. "That was a long time ago. Until 1944, we deep fried 'pooris' only in pure ghee," she said.

some menus as guidelines

1
Steamed rice
Chintha chiguru pappu *p. 57*
Carrot pachchadi *p. 12*
Karivēpāku podi *p. 23*
Theeyati pulusu *p. 60*
Vankāya vēpudu *p. 49*
Crispies, pickle, curd, sweet

2
Steamed rice
Pālakoora pappu *p. 53*
Vankāya pachchadi *p. 4*
Kandhi podi *p. 25*
Chāru *p. 61*
Any vēpudu *p. 49*
Crispies, pickle, curd, sweet

3
Steamed rice
Sāmbār *p. 58*
Pālakoora pachchadi *p. 3*
Podi chutney *p. 22*
Theeyati chāru *p. 62*
Peddha chikkudukāya koora *p. 46*
Crispies, pickle, curd, sweet

4
Steamed rice
Pindimiriyam *p. 59*
Kobbarikāya pachchadi *p. 10*
Nuvvulu podi *p. 21*
Aratidhoota perugu pachchadi *p. 67*
Beerakāya koora *ref. p. 27*
Crispies, pickle, curd, sweet

5
Steamed rice
Ākukoora majjiga pulusu *p. 66*
Gōngoora pachchadi *p. 15*
Podi chutney *p. 22*
Any vēpudu *p. 49*
Crispies, pickle, curd, sweet

6
Bisi bele huli *p. 33*
Any perugu pachchadi *p. 67*
Dhadhyōdhanam *p. 37*
Crispies, pickle

7
Vāngi bāth *p. 34*
Any perugu pachchadi *p. 67*
Steamed rice
Chāru *p. 61*
Dhadhyōdhanam *p. 37*
Crispies, pickle

a word about Andhra cuisine

Fluffy, white, steaming rice with an array of spicy, tasty accompaniments - this is what a typical Andhra meal looks like. Most accompaniments are mixed into rice with a dash of warm ghee or oil. In this book, these accompaniments have been broadly classified into: Pachchadi (chutneys), Podi (powders), Pappu (dals) and Koora (vegetables). The Andhra Chāru (rasam) is included in the section on dals. Then there is 'Pulusu' which is generally a thick sour gravy, either using tamarind - Theeyati pulusu (p. 60) or yogurt - Majjiga pulusu (p. 65).

a typical Andhra meal

Steamed rice as the staple

Main accompaniments: pappu, pachchadi, podi

One or two side-dishes like koora, vēpudu or pulusu

Some crispies, pickle, curd / curd rice

On special occasions, a special rice and a sweet dish

a festive menu (picture on facing page)

RICE: Steamed rice, Pulihōrā *p. 35*, Dhadhyōdhanam *p. 37*
POWDERS: Podi chutney *p. 22*, Karivēpāku podi *p. 23*
CHUTNEYS: Carrot pachchadi *p. 12*, Ullipāya pachchadi *p. 11*
DALS: Majjiga pulusu *p. 65*, Tamātā pappu *p. 56*, Chāru *p. 61*, Pālakoora pappu *p. 53*
VEGETABLES: Pātōli *p. 48*, Aratidhoota koora *p. 43*
SWEETS: Bādām pāyasam *p. 72*, Ravva kēsari *p.75*, Minapasunni *p. 76*
Poppadams, pickle, fresh homemade ghee
Bananas, betel leaves and betel nuts

This is an elaborate and festive meal
that holds special memories for Pedatha
- her father's favourites in his very own plate.
(menu on facing page)

English
Telugu
Hindi

a visual glossary of select ingredients placed diagonally in alphabetical order

1. Amaranth leaves
Thōtakoora
Chauli ka saag
Mula keerai in Tamil

4. Beaten rice
Atukulu
Poha

9. Brinjal (bharta variety)
Peddha vankāya
Bharta baingan

16. Cluster beans
Gōru chikkudukāya
Gawarphali

3. Banana stem
Aratidhoota
Kele ka tana

8. Bottle gourd
Ānapakāya
Lauki

15. Clarified butter
Neyyi
Ghee

21. Coriander seeds
Dhaniyālu
Dhaniya

2. Asafoetida
Inguva
Hing

7. Black-eyed beans
Bobbarlu
Lobiya

14. Carom seeds
Vāmu
Ajwain

20. Coriander leaves/Cilantro
Kothimeeri
Hara dhaniya

6. Bitter gourd
Kākarakāya
Karela

13. Cardamom (green)
Elakkāya
Elaichi

12. Capsicum
Butta mirapa
Shimla mirch

19. Cooking camphor
Pachakarpooram
Kapoor

24. Drumstick
Mulagakāya
Saijan ki phali

5. Bengal gram
Senaga pappu
Chane ki dal

11. Broad beans
Chikkudukāya

18. Chillies
Mirapa
Mirchi

23. Curry leaves
Karivēpāku
Kari patte

10. Brinjal/Aubergine
Vankāya
Baingan

17. Coconut
Kobbarikāya
Nariyal

22. Cumin seeds
Jeelakarra
Jeera

25. Dry coconut
Endu kobbarikāya
Khopra

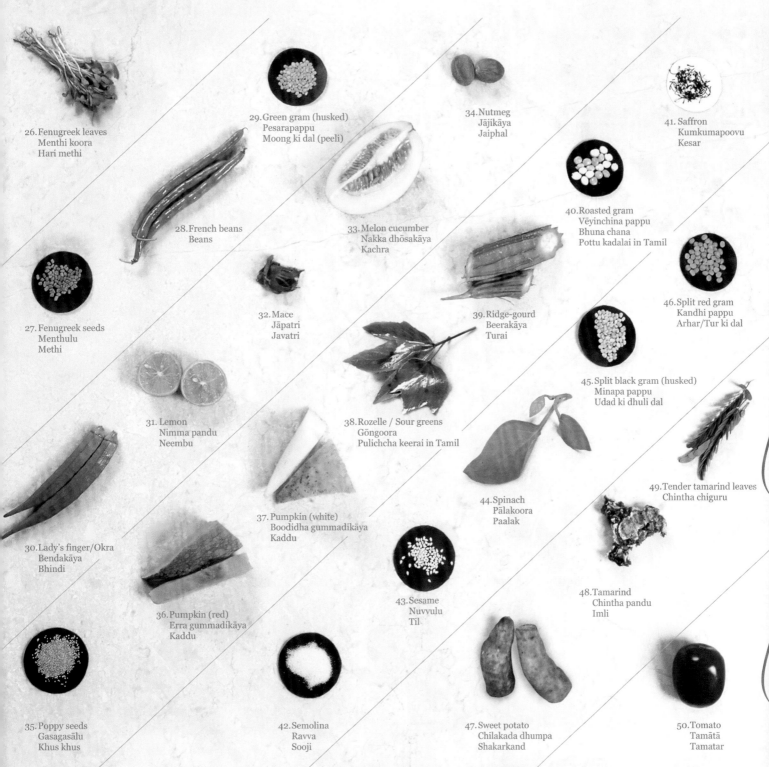

26. Fenugreek leaves
    Menthi koora
    Hari methi

27. Fenugreek seeds
    Menthulu
    Methi

28. French beans
    Beans

29. Green gram (husked)
    Pesarapappu
    Moong ki dal (peeli)

30. Lady's finger/Okra
    Bendakāya
    Bhindi

31. Lemon
    Nimma pandu
    Neembu

32. Mace
    Jāpatri
    Javatri

33. Melon cucumber
    Nakka dhōsakāya
    Kachra

34. Nutmeg
    Jājikāya
    Jaiphal

35. Poppy seeds
    Gasagasālu
    Khus khus

36. Pumpkin (red)
    Erra gummadikāya
    Kaddu

37. Pumpkin (white)
    Boodidha gummadikāya
    Kaddu

38. Rozelle / Sour greens
    Gōngoora
    Pulichcha keerai in Tamil

39. Ridge-gourd
    Beerakāya
    Turai

40. Roasted gram
    Vēyinchina pappu
    Bhuna chana
    Pottu kadalai in Tamil

41. Saffron
    Kumkumapoovu
    Kesar

42. Semolina
    Ravva
    Sooji

43. Sesame
    Nuvvulu
    Til

44. Spinach
    Pālakoora
    Paalak

45. Split black gram (husked)
    Minapa pappu
    Udad ki dhuli dal

46. Split red gram
    Kandhi pappu
    Arhar/Tur ki dal

47. Sweet potato
    Chilakada dhumpa
    Shakarkand

48. Tamarind
    Chintha pandu
    Imli

49. Tender tamarind leaves
    Chintha chiguru

50. Tomato
    Tamātā
    Tamatar

her snow-white hair
kind and calm eyes
her old voice, strong and sure
resonates once more
as she echoes her mother's voice

she speaks and we write
a teaspoon of mustard
a cup of rice
roast until the gram turns golden

words are recorded
and the recipes learnt
all of them

but...
cooking, everyone knows
is not ingredients precise
nor merely a technique
it is an intuition
a flavour, a whiff...

the gram turning rose-red
the aroma of popping mustard
a pinch of saffron
a fist-full of rice
and much much more
the hand that feeds
the smile that twinkles
the wisdom of years
her years of wisdom

how do we capture these?

annadaata sukhi bhava